From King
to Obama:
Witness to a
Turbulent History

A Memoir

by Earl Ofari Hutchinson

http://www.4earlofarihutchinson.com

Book Design – Shri Henkel
Cover Design – Alan Ball

Martin Luther King photo: Walter P. Reuther Library, Archives of Labor and Urban Affairs, Wayne State University.
Barack Obama photo: Associated Press.

Library of Congress Cataloging-in-Publication data for this title is available from the Library of Congress

Hutchinson, Earl Ofari.
    From King to Obama : witness to a turbulent history / Earl Ofari Hutchinson.
    249 pages cm
    Includes index.

    ISBN 978-0692370711

    1. Hutchinson, Earl Ofari. 2. Journalists--United States--Biography. 3. Political activists--United States--Biography. 4. African Americans--History--1964-
5. United States--Politics and government--20th century.
6. United States--Politics and government--21st century.
I. Title.

PN4874.H88A3 2015   070.92
                QBI15-600017

Contents

Acknowledgments

My son-in-law, Stephen Kelly, first floated the idea of a memoir. He prodded me over the months to put pen to paper and tell about my experiences over the decades as a writer, broadcaster and activist.

Then I saw the biopic *Get on Up*, on James Brown. I constantly read about other biopics in the works on Marvin Gaye, Miles Davis, Nina Simone, and Jimi Hendrix not to mention the many documentaries on the Panthers, the civil rights movements, and the Vietnam War. This spurred me to finally sit down and list the names of the many personalities who I had either interviewed, had conversations with, or covered events or performances of theirs.

Yvonne Divans Hutchinson, and my daughter Sikivu Hutchinson offered critical insights into key sections of the book. My son Fanon Hutchinson produced the companion video of the book.

The Southern California Library for Social Studies and Research are the custodian of my personal papers, The Earl Ofari Hutchinson Collection. The library under the able tutelage of Yusef Omawale and Michele Welsing, was of invaluable assistance in the research and helpful direction of this work.

A special thanks also to Reverend Al Sharpton, Congresswoman Maxine Waters, L.A. City Councilman Bernard Parks, L.A. City Councilman Herb Wesson, L.A. Mayor Eric Garcetti, Bishop Charles Blake, Pastor Kelvin Sauls, Jonathan Weedman, Wells Fargo Foundation, Alva Mason, Toyota Foundation, and Weingart Foundation Official, Steve Soboroff. They have also been great sources of support.

A special thanks must go to the staff of KPFK and Pacifica Radio, Gerardo Borrego, KTYM Radio, Pluria Marshall and Don Wanlass at the *L.A. Wave Newspaper*, the New America Media and its founder and my long-time friend Sandy Close, Beverly Smith founder host of the Bev Smith Show, Arianna Huffington, *The Huffington Post*, Dan Wood at the *Christian Science Monitor*, Ron Childs formerly of the *Chicago Defender*, Tamron Hall and the producers at MSNBC, Fatyn Muhammad, WLIB, Mark Thompson, Sirius XM,

From King to Obama: Witness to a Turbulent History would not be possible without the superb design, technical production and promotion of Nikki Leigh and Alan Ball.

Finally, it would not be possible without the strength and encouragement Barbara Bramwell, my wife, has given me in all of my writing projects and much more through the years. She was the driving force behind the publishing company, *Middle Passage Press*, we founded. She has been my loving helpmate, travel companion, and comfort. This has made a huge difference in my work. I love her deeply for this and much more. She, and the others, has been there for me through my journey. I thank them all.

Books by Earl Ofari Hutchinson

How Obama Won

How Obama Governed

The Ethnic Presidency: How Race decides the Race to the White House

The Latino Challenge to Black America

The Crisis in Black and Black

The Assassination of the Black Male Image

Beyond O.J.: Race, Sex and Class Lessons for America

Blacks and Reds: Race and Class in Conflict 1919-1990

Betrayed: A History of Presidential Failure to Protect Black Lives

Prescript - Coming of Age in America

It was May 31, 1964. I was 18 and my father said that he'd like for me to go with him to an event at the Los Angeles Memorial Coliseum. He said it would be an event that I would long remember. He was right. It was one of those pitch perfect spring days in Los Angeles with a slight morning overcast haze that at that time of the year always burned off by mid-day.

When we pulled into the Coliseum parking lot, I was immediately struck by the size and bustle of the throng that streamed through the gates. It looked like a little United Nations. There were whites, blacks, Asians, and Hispanics. Many of those who rushed by me wore clerical collars, and priestly garments. This was fitting since I noted that there were a large number of priests and nuns among the crowd. They were readily recognizable and familiar to me in their garb. For nine years I had attended two Catholic elementary schools and then Mt. Carmel High school in my freshman year. The schools were on Chicago's South Side.

I realized that this was an event that was special and that it had to do with civil rights. The scenes of blacks marching, picketing, and being assaulted by club welding Southern cops, and Confederate flag-waving white toughs, had become commonplace viewing on the nightly news in 1964. The scenes were jarringly etched into my consciousness. The names of the civil rights battlegrounds had become almost household names; Jackson, Mississippi, Birmingham, Alabama, St. Augustine,

Florida, Albany, Georgia, and Greensboro, North Carolina. A year earlier, Mississippi NAACP field director Medgar Evers was gunned down in Jackson and the shooter was a white Citizens Council member, Byron de la Beckwith. After two trials, an all-white jury refused to convict him. This was standard fare then when civil rights workers were maimed or killed. Southern white juries, with rare exceptions, never convicted them.

Though I was a high school student in Los Angeles then, the one name that had become the watchword for the civil rights struggle was Dr. Martin Luther King, Jr. His name was constantly mentioned with reverence by my parents. The event my father was determined that I attend with him was billed as a "Religious Witness for Human Dignity." I knew from the many religious types who were in the crowd this was a multi-faith event. Shortly after being seated, all eyes turned to the main Coliseum tunnel entrance. I had played high school football and had attended several L.A. Rams games. In those days the Rams played their home games at the Coliseum. The Rams players had burst through this tunnel onto the playing field. It wasn't the Rams that emerged from the tunnel that day, though. Instead, there was a slow procession of priests, rabbis, and protestant ministers that marched solemnly out of the tunnel onto the Coliseum running track. The crowd immediately roared when they marched into view.

All eyes were immediately locked on the small, short, nattily-dressed man at the head of the procession. Despite the processional's somber mood, the man whom everyone intently watched, smiled broadly and waved to the cheering crowd. We were seated in the front section near the railing. Like many others in the crowd, I stared at Dr. King with a mix of awe and wonderment. This smallish man was the unrivaled symbol of a movement which had grown to global importance and dominated the talk at dinner tables in millions of homes. It also stirred much talk, debate and rancor in many statehouses especially in the South, the halls of Congress and the White House. The debate over civil rights had at once both divided and united blacks and whites as no other cause had done in decades.

*****

I personally don't remember much of what Dr. King told the gathering that day. I do remember that he spoke from a lectern in the center of the playing field. Behind him, there sat a row of black and white ministers. King's speech that day was not lost. A digitized version of his forty-minute address was unearthed in January 2013. It has been carefully preserved in the archives at Pepperdine University.

I remembered, though, that nine months earlier, on August 28, 1963, I watched on TV as he electrified the crowd estimated at a quarter million in Washington D.C. and the nation with his " I Have a Dream" speech. Almost certainly, he struck many of the same themes in his speech that day; the fight against segregation, poverty, the battle for civil rights, a reiteration of his commitment to non-violent resistance. These were the staple themes in all of his speeches. The rally at the Coliseum came little more than a month before the passage of the 1964 civil rights bill, on July 2. I'm sure that King implored the crowd to put fire under Congress to end the infuriating and dogged filibuster that rabid Southern Democrats and Northern GOP conservatives used to bottle up the bill.

There was a heightened sense of urgency that day as King spoke that Congress needed one more big push to break the filibuster and pass the landmark bill. King's appearance at the Coliseum was designed to further provide that impetus. It was part of his national swing to rally support and public opinion and to enlist the support of religious leaders in that battle. As it turned out, his speech at the Coliseum that late May Day would prove invaluable as a means of rallying support in Los Angeles for civil rights. As the rally ended, the crowd joined in a lusty, full throated singing of the movement's anthem, "We Shall Overcome." I joined in too. I knew as I stood at almost arms-length from King as he walked past me on the track that I, along with the thousands of others in the Coliseum that day, had been witness to the making of another signal event in history.

*****

The 1960s has been called by historians the decade of change. It was that. In Greensboro, North Carolina, four black students begin a sit-in at a segregated Woolworth's lunch counter. Although they were refused service, they were allowed to stay at the counter. The event triggered many similar nonviolent protests throughout the Southern United States, and 6 months later the original 4 protesters were served lunch at the same counter. The Vietnam War officially began. President Kennedy was assassinated. Martin Luther King, Jr. issues his "Letter from Birmingham Jail".

The Beatles held the top 5 positions in the Billboard Top 40 singles in America, an unprecedented achievement. 34 people died in the Watts riot. 32,000 people made a 54-mile "freedom march" from Selma to Montgomery. Four black girls are killed. Martin Luther King Jr. Made his "I Have a Dream" Speech. Muhammad Ali won the heavy weight championship title and announced he's a Black Muslim. The Civil Rights Act Passed in the U.S. Nelson Mandela was sentenced to Life in Prison. There were mass Draft Protests in the U.S. Thurgood Marshall became the First African-American U.S. Supreme Court Justice. Robert F. Kennedy was assassinated.

The 1970s were no less eventful. The Kent State University shootings happened. The Watergate Scandal began. Roe vs Wade Legalizes Abortion in the U.S. President Nixon Resigned in disgrace rather than face impeachment and there was the Jim Jones People Temple massacre.

*****

The common thread in my eyewitness view of and engagement with the pivotal personalities and events of the time is the civil rights and black movements of the mid 1960s onward.

A short chronology is in order.

James Meredith became the first black student to enroll at the University of Mississippi. Violence and riots surrounding the incident caused President Kennedy to send 5,000 federal troops. During civil rights protests in Birmingham, Ala., Commissioner of Public Safety Eugene "Bull" Connor used fire hoses and police dogs on black demonstrators. These images of brutality, which are televised and published widely, were instrumental in gaining sympathy for the civil rights movement around the world.

About 200,000 people joined the March on Washington. They congregated at the Lincoln Memorial. The participants listened to Martin Luther King deliver his famous "I Have a Dream" speech.

Four young girls (Denise McNair, Cynthia Wesley, Carole Robertson, and Addie Mae Collins) attending Sunday school were killed when a bomb explodes at the Sixteenth Street Baptist Church in Birmingham, Alabama. The church was a popular location for civil rights meetings. Riots erupted in Birmingham, leading to the deaths of two more black youths.

The Council of Federated Organizations (COFO), a network of civil rights groups that included CORE and SNCC, launched a massive effort to register black voters during what became known as the Freedom Summer. It also sent delegates to the Democratic National Convention to protest—and attempt to unseat—the official all-white Mississippi contingent.

President Johnson signed the Civil Rights Act of 1964. The most sweeping civil rights legislation since Reconstruction, the Civil Rights Act prohibited discrimination of all kinds based on race, color, religion, or national origin. The law provided the federal government with the powers to enforce desegregation.

The bodies of three civil-rights workers—two white, one black—were found in an earthen dam, six weeks into a federal investigation backed by President Johnson. James E. Chaney, 21; Andrew Goodman, 21; and Michael Schwerner, 24, worked to register black voters in Mississippi, and, on June 21, had gone to investigate the burning of a black church. They were arrested by the police on speeding charges, incarcerated for several hours, and then released after dark into the hands of the Ku Klux Klan, who murdered them.

Malcolm X, black nationalist and founder of the Organization of Afro-American Unity, was shot to death. It is believed the assailants were members of the Black Muslim faith, which Malcolm had recently abandoned in favor of orthodox Islam.

Blacks began a march to Montgomery in support of voting rights. They were stopped at the Edmund Pettus Bridge by a police blockade. Fifty marchers were hospitalized after police used tear gas, whips, and clubs against them. The incident was dubbed "Bloody Sunday" by the media. The march was considered the catalyst for pushing through the voting rights act five months later.

Congress passed the Voting Rights Act of 1965 that made it easier for Southern blacks to register to vote. Literacy tests, poll taxes, and other such requirements that were used to restrict black voting were made illegal.

Race riots erupted in a black section of Los Angeles. President Johnson issued Executive Order 11246, which enforced affirmative action for the first time. It required government contractors to "take affirmative action" toward prospective minority employees in all aspects of hiring and employment.

The Black Panthers were founded by Huey Newton and Bobby Seale.

Stokely Carmichael, a leader of the Student Nonviolent Coordinating Committee (SNCC), coined the phrase "black power" in a speech in Seattle.

Major race riots take place in Newark (July 12–16) and Detroit (July 23–30).

Martin Luther King, at age 39, was shot as he stood on the balcony outside his hotel room. Escaped convict and committed racist James Earl Ray was convicted of the crime.

President Johnson signed the Civil Rights Act of 1968, prohibiting discrimination in the sale, rental, and financing of housing.

The Supreme Court, in *Swann* v. *Charlotte-Mecklenburg Board of Education*, upheld bussing as a mean to insure school integration.

Overriding President Reagan's veto, Congress passed the Civil Rights Restoration Act, which expanded the reach of non-discrimination laws within private institutions receiving federal funds.

After two years of debates, vetoes, and threatened vetoes, **President**

Bush reversed himself and signed the Civil Rights Act of 1991, strengthening existing civil rights laws and providing for damages in cases of intentional employment discrimination. The first race riots in decades erupt in south-central Los Angeles after a jury acquitted four white police officers for the videotaped beating of African American Rodney King.

This was the time that I came of age in America and became deeply involved in writing about, doing broadcasts on, conducting interviews, and participating in many of the pivotal events during those decades. My involvement in, and reporting of, these events and the important figures that shaped them didn't end in at the end of the 1970s. I continued my reporting on, and engagement with history makers and shapers in the 1980s and 1990s and into the 21st Century. The pivotal figures of these eras make up my witness to a turbulent history too.

Introduction - The Retina of a Turbulent History

I thought of the oft repeated quip from composer Igor Stravinsky when I decided to write my eyewitness account of a turbulent history. He was 11-years-old when he caught his only glimpse of the Russian composer Peter Ilyich Tchaikovsky at intermission at a performance of Mikhail Glinka's *Ruslan and Lyudmila* in 1893. Stravinsky was so thrilled at seeing the giant of classical composition in person that he would say until the end of his life that that image "remained in the retina of my memory all my life." I felt exactly the same way in writing this remembrance of the past and of those who history now regards as major influential figures.

The great challenge in writing a history of the people and events that remain firmly in the retina of my memory and of whom I had the phenomenal fortune to have seen, heard, talked with, interviewed and have been in their presence is to convey to the reader the tremendous sense of importance I felt at walking in the shadow of history when I was in their presence. My mission is to convey the feeling I had about the people and places that affected my life and the lives of millions.

This is not an autobiography. The lines are often blurred between a memoir and an autobiography. But, there is a clear difference between the two. An autobiography by definition focuses on the trajectory of a person's entire life. It has an even flow. It generally presents dates, places, and times in sequential order. It purports to be an honest, factual narrative of a person's life and work. A memoir is looser, more intimate, and, above all, intensely personal. The people and the events depicted can be ordered and reordered, scrambled, shifted, and moved around in any way the writer wants that suits to add drama to the narrative and breathe life into the impressions he or she had of them.

This is simply my personal impressions and remembrances of the many individuals I interviewed, saw at events, and of the actions that I was a part of, observed up close, over a half century. I did this first as a child selling Christmas cards in 1958, then in the mid-1960s attending events with my father, and in the late 1960s as an activist in a campus Black Student Union. I backed into them later when I got a job by sheer luck. I saw a help wanted ad in the newspaper, needed a job, and on a whim applied even though I had no experience as a reporter and journalist. The job was a reporter and feature writer at the *Los Angeles Free Press* from 1971 to 1973. After that I worked for nearly a decade as a news and public affairs producer and broadcaster at KPFK radio. For three decades after that, I worked as an author, radio and TV communicator and activist.

In addition to political events and issues, I also had a deep interest in the film, music, and the sports scene during those decades. Part of my task as a reporter for the *Los Angeles Free Press*, and afterwards as a public affairs producer for Pacifica Radio in Los Angeles and host of a weekly talk show at the station was to cover arts and sports events. My tape recorder was always in hand and I scrupulously tried to capture their words and thoughts about their work on tape.

The Free Press, or the *Freep*, as it was commonly called was the brainchild of Art Kunkin who had cut his teeth in the Socialist movement of two decades earlier. The paper was one of the most widely distributed so-called underground newspapers of the 1960s. It is often cited as one of the first such newspapers. This made it by default the watchword in arts and entertainment coverage in L.A. This assured that I could get access and interviews with many of the major progressive and popular artists then. Even when that wasn't possible, I almost always got press tickets to attend their concerts and appearances.

There were other occasions when I had chance encounters on the street or in other public venues with a noted figure. The names of the movers and shakers in the arts and sports scene during those years fill the pages of dozens of biographies, articles and subject of movies and documentaries. There's Mahalia Jackson, the Beatles, Bob Marley, Alex Haley, Miles Davis, Jimi Hendrix, Nina Simone, Miriam Makeba, Ray Charles, Richard Pryor, Eartha Kitt, Paul Winfield, Muhammad Ali, Wilt Chamberlain and Rachel and Jackie Robinson and Sugar Ray Robinson. I either interviewed or reported on a film, concert, sporting event, or just plain had occasion to see them in a venue. They are fitting compliments to the political, civil rights, and social activist personalities that I engaged with at one time or another over the past half century. There are many other notables that I also engaged with in a variety of ways but did not include here. The reason for that is simple. They are still alive. They may well figure into a future narrative.

From King to Obama: Witness to a Turbulent History is not an exhaustive, in depth, definitive, or even a timeline of my engagement with the major personalities and the important events from the mid-1960s into the first two decades of the 21st Century. However, nearly all of the personalities that I paint a personal picture of have attained legendary status; in some cases they have become household names. They have been the subject of biopic movies made or that are in the process of being made about their lives.

*****

I wanted this to be a fast paced, highly readable, and enjoyable remembrance that gives a sweeping feel of the times. Further, I make no pretense that this is a definitive study of a half century of eventful change in America and the world. This would be presumptuous and arrogant. There have been mountains of historical and political studies and autobiographies and personal chronicles that sift through all the events, developments and the personalities of the half century I chronicle in minute detail. This is especially true of the 1960s and the civil rights movement.

One need look no further than David Halberstam's, *The Fifties*, David Farber's, *The Age of Great Dreams: America in the 1960s*, David Frum's, *How We Got Here: The 70s The Decade That Brought You Modern Life -- For Better Or Worst*, David Sirota's, *Back to Our Future: How the 1980s Explain the World We Live in Now--Our Culture, Our Politics, Our Everything*. There are books on the 1990s by Alan Binder and Janet Yellen, *The Fabulous Decade: Macroeconomic Lessons from the 1990s*, and Robert T. Kyosaki's, *The Business of the 21st Century*.

I'm also aware that a personal perspective on noted figures and events is always open to many other interpretations. Thousands of others have also known these individuals far more intimately than I ever could. These were their wives, husbands, sons, and daughters, friends, agents, writers, producers, business partners, professional associates and co-workers. This is solely my reflections on the individuals and events that span a half century.

It's a remembrance of the way they impressed me. I had to make choices, many choices, about what and how to relate my experiences, taking special care to be as honest and accurate in relating those experiences as possible.

In this respect I took a cue from the eminent British historian E.H. Carr. In his definitive work, *What is History*, he wrote: "History begins with the handing down of tradition; and tradition means the carrying of the habits and lessons of the past into the future. Records of the past begin to be kept for the benefit of future generations." He was partially right. But it's more than recording dry dates, places, and people and events when recounting that history. The task is to bring it alive, inject passion and fire into it. Paint a vivid picture of the pageant of history.

I had a great well-spring of people and events to draw from. I had the tumultuous decades of the 1960s and 1970s. This was the time that I came of social and political age in America. I bore witness to those events and the success of those historic personalities as a journalist, broadcaster, and activist. At times, I rubbed shoulders almost literally with many of them while being a participant in the key events of that era.

My aim is in part to write first about the impressions I have of those people and events. Then give a personal glimpse of their impact on my life. Finally, I aim to place them against the backdrop of the profound social, artistic, and political changes in America and the world.

In writing a personal account of people and purposeful events, I seek to humanize my experiences with, observations of, and discussions with them. I am guided by Carr's view that history must be both interpretation and personal perspective if it is to have any real meaning. He noted that history has been called a "hard core of facts" surrounded by a "pulp of disputable interpretation." The operative word in that interpretation is to make history resonate and ultimately stick in the reader's consciousness. A memoir and reflections on people, places and things that one has known or has first-hand knowledge of should tell why and how things happened as they did. It should tell why the memories of people and events that have been plucked out of one's past experience should have special importance. And they tell why the particular elements that make up one's past are important.

One example among the many chronicled in my memoir is the book signing in 1976 I attended with *Roots* author Alex Haley. *Roots* was a global phenomenon. *Roots* had solid historical interest because of the missing piece it sewed together about one black American's successful attempt to trace his hitherto blotted out family genealogy back to its African source. This was not just an historical occurrence. Haley's rendering of his family saga plucked a deep nerve and affected so many other African-Americans precisely because their family history was a blank page. Many of them longed to discover that history. That's why hundreds of people waited for hours in a line at a small bookstore and community center in South L.A. to see, greet, and have their book signed by him. Haley performed a miracle of historical story telling. I wanted my eyewitness remembrance to do the same.

It is more than history or interpretation. It is my effort to make that history a joy to read.

I am also mindful that personal impressions and reflections on important events and personalities have to be more than just a compilation of personal anecdotes. They also must be based on factual information and accounts of individual's lives and the events that are being described. They must of necessity draw on varied sources. such as government documents, personal letters, diaries, and oral histories. Next the job is to stitch them together in a coherent whole.

Any memoir also must be selective in its focus. That is certainly true with my eyewitness account. As with anyone who has lived a long, rich and varied life, trying to decide what and who were the most significant events and persons in one's life, and thus what to choose in a remembrance, is like choosing food at a smorgasbord. They present a storehouse of historical culinary delights to pick from. As with any discerning diner, one is forced to make choices. I had to do the same in this book. The checklist of persons I saw and interviewed and the events I witnessed is long. Many did not make the final cut.

There was my attendance at the 1984 Olympic Games in Los Angeles and my attendance at the 2000 Democratic Convention in Los Angeles. There was Pope John Paul II's visit to L.A. in September, 1987. There was the assignment I gave to a co-worker to cover the Michael Jackson child molestation trial in February, 2005. She provided the most complete day-to-day coverage of the courtroom drama. There was the birthday celebration for my father, Earl Hutchinson, Sr., in 2003. It was his 100th birthday. The celebration was hailed by President Bill Clinton. This was preceded by a day of recognition of him by the Los Angeles City Council. His wife Dorothy Hutchinson, and friends, and varied political officials attended. It coincided with the publication of his book, *A Colored Man's Journey Through 20th Century Segregated America.*

There was the stunning revelation by Essie Mae Washington-Williams in 2003 that she was the daughter of one-time arch segregationist South Carolina senator Strom Thurmond. This revelation literally hit home. A year earlier at a July 4th fire-works event at the Los Angeles Coliseum, her grand-daughter, Maria Hutchinson, my son, Fanon's wife, casually said to me that Ms. Washington-Williams was Thurmond's daughter and that she would soon go public with that revelation.

In December 2003, in Columbia, South Carolina, she faced a bank of news cameras and told the world that she was Thurmond's daughter. I would share many family gatherings with her. On occasion we talked about her relations with Thurmond. She revealed much about it in her best-selling book, *Dear Senator: A Memoir by the Daughter of Strom Thurmond.* I hosted a live book signing and discussion for and with her in Los Angeles after the book's release.

Then there were my travels. In three decades I traveled to 27 countries in Europe, Asia, Africa, Latin America, the Caribbean, and Canada. I toured the major world renowned historical and cultural building and sights in these countries. In addition, I have authored eleven books. Through the years I have traveled to every major city in the United States on speaking engagements, book signings, and covering events.

*****

There's another note on this work. I present my remembrance as a personal series of vignettes and impressions of those whom I met, interviewed, or heard speak at events. With the exception of Rachel Robinson, Muhammad Ali, James Meredith, O.J. Simpson, and Special Assistant to President Obama, Valerie Jarrett, and President Obama, all of the individuals in the book have passed away. Robinson, Meredith, Ali, Simpson, Jarrett and Obama are the exceptions because of their connection to the seismic and defining moments in American history. In the case of Ali, it is the shock he caused when he joined the Black Muslims and his subsequent stance against the Vietnam War.

With Rachel Robinson it was her dedication to preserving the legacy of her husband, Jackie Robinson. With Johnny Cochran, it is the commanding role he played in the O.J. Simpson case and other major legal battles. Meredith had attained a historic first in integrating the University of Mississippi and the bloody historic bloody confrontation between the U.S. Government and a Southern state. Rachel and

Cochran apart from Jackie and the Simpson case are compelling figures with compelling stories in their own right. President Obama and Jarrett are included because of their history making importance and because of Obama's historic link to King.

My goal in *From King to Obama: Witness to a Turbulent History:* is to give the reader a real sense of the profound human drama of the big events, major personalities, and the issues that changed America in the second half of the 20th Century and the first decade of the 21st Century. This is the retina of my life's memory.

Chapter 1
Their Eyes Were
on the Prize

Chapter 1 - Their Eyes Were on the Prize

The staff at the *Los Angeles Free Press* was excited in October 1972 when they got word that United Farmworkers of America's founder and President Cesar Chavez would be stopping by our offices. I was a bit on edge because I was assigned to interview him. My edginess stemmed in part from fear, and in part awe of him.

Chavez had focused public attention on the exploitation and desperate plight of the men and women who picked the nation's fruits and vegetables in blazing heat and biting cold in the fields. They worked for near slave wages, were subject to threats, intimidation, abuse, and even violence. The overwhelming majority of them in the Western states were undocumented workers from Mexico. The growers shuffled around at will from field to field and when the crop was harvested often dumped them back across the Mexican border.

Chavez, like Dr. King, was not just the head of an organization dedicated to fighting for fair wages and better working conditions for the farmworkers. He was a pivotal and inspirational figure in the civil rights and labor reform movement. What made the interview even more exciting was that Chavez was coming to the *Free Press* offices. In anticipation of that and to make sure I had my facts straight, I read numerous news accounts, and stories about Chavez and the United Farmworkers. I was deeply conscious that I would be sitting in the same room with a true movement giant.

My first surprise came when Chavez arrived at the offices. He had no entourage, companions, or bodyguards. It was just him and a young aide. He greeted me with a broad smile and warm embrace as if we were old friends who had known each other for years. There was absolutely no air, pretense or assumed importance about him. He was the paragon of modesty and humility. He spoke softly, and in deliberate tones, and he chose his words very carefully.

During the roughly one hour that we talked, Chavez ranged over many of the issues that were crucial to the farmworkers and their drive to unionize; the low wages, the back breaking labor, the often harsh treatment they were subjected to, the lack of sanitary facilities. Chavez always set this against the guns and clubs that he and union organizers routinely faced from grower sponsored assailants. They were determined to beat back the farmworkers in their long and bitter fight for better wages and working conditions.

Chavez eagerly praised Dr. King. He made it plain that King was his hero and that he patterned himself and his activist, aggressive emphasis on non-violence after King's actions. Chavez beamed every time he mentioned King. He mentioned him often. He had a near devout gaze as he recalled to me the telegram that he had received from him in September 1966, in which King wrote, "You and your valiant fellow workers have demonstrated your commitment to righting grievous wrongs forced upon exploited people." Chavez made clear that he had regarded King as his teacher and they shared much in common in the tactics and goals they employed.

It was a great moment for me listening to Chavez pay tribute testament to King. He rose slowly at the end of the interview and walked slowly to the outer office. He paused for a moment, quietly thanked me, and shook my hand warmly. As I watched him leave the full impact of being in his presence hit me. The reality that I had sat a few feet from this humble, but powerful figure, gave me an intense feeling of pride. It was the same feeling that I got six years earlier when I stood just a few feet from Dr. King at a rally of religious leaders for civil rights at the L.A. Coliseum.

King and Chavez! I had seen and heard both, up close. Now I knew why these two giants in the fight for justice and equality had a symbiotic bond and kinship. Their names were linked together and I was sure the relationship of the two men, their ideals, and their fight, would stand the test of time. It was indeed a true mark and testament to their work that both would be honored with holidays in their name. The national holiday for King comes the third week of January. Chavez is honored with a state holiday in California on March 31, and an optional holiday in states such as Colorado and Texas. Celebrations for him are held in many other parts of the nation.

I saw and heard Chavez several times over the next few years. Nothing had changed from the day he sat across from me in the small office at the newspaper for the interview. I was always moved by the warmth, humility and soft spoken measured manner in which he spoke. The burning passion and conviction and absolute iron determination he had to win justice and equal treatment for the farmworkers.

Following his death in April, 1993, his widow donated his black nylon union jacket to the National Museum of American History which is a branch of the Smithsonian. He was 66. This was the same jacket that Chavez had with him when he came to the *Free Press* offices for our interview two decades earlier. The jacket symbolized his and the farmworker's quest to advance the cause of social justice in America. Now it belonged to the nation.

*****

In 1972 the great battles against segregation in the 1960s had largely ended with the passage of the 1964 Civil Rights Act and the 1965 Voting Rights Act and a slew of other civil rights initiatives. But the old, well-known veterans of the civil rights movement had not faded away. Inevitably when one of them would come to L.A., I would get the assignment to do an interview with and a profile on them. There was always a tinge of nervousness and excitement when that happened. That was the case when I sat in the lobby of a hotel, in April, 1972, in Century City waiting to be escorted up to the room where I would interview Ralph David Abernathy. A day before he had spoken at an anti-war rally at the Embassy Auditorium near downtown Los Angeles. I covered the rally. He urged the crowd to make "a non-violent seizure of power." He quickly added that the way to do that was through increased electoral involvement.

Abernathy was nearly as famed as Dr. King. He and King had been virtually joined at the hip through countless marches, rallies, protests, and sharing jail cells, in nearly every hot spot in the South from 1955 to

1968. Abernathy tallied a mind boggling 44 arrests and daily death threats against his life and those of his wife and children. Abernathy was there on the balcony at the Lorraine Motel in Memphis when King was gunned down in April, 1968, Undaunted, he seemed determined to keep their organization, the Southern Christian Leadership Conference, intact.

Abernathy greeted me expansively when I entered his suite. I was fascinated as he spoke with a deep sonorous tone, and slow drawl. Beyond the fact that he carried the official mantle of King, he further endeared himself to me when he paused, eyed me curiously, and said "And you're the writer." It was less a question than I hoped a compliment. However it was intended, the question which really wasn't a question instantly boosted my self-esteem. For a moment, I felt pushed to a rarified spot in the literary world; the world of the recognized writer. And now Abernathy had in one breath validated me. I was on cloud nine.

The interview was relatively brief. Several times an aide would come in and whisper something to him. I got the sense that time was of the essence to them, and that they were going to observe a strict time limit in talking to me. I didn't push it by asking too many questions when Abernathy and his associates had their internal time limit set for me.

Yet, I felt he did cover the standard talking points about SCLC, his plans for it, and the issues that the organization would stress in the future. Abernathy answered the questions I posed in that slow drawl. He emphasized that he was not overwhelmed by the task of keeping a national organization together that was borne on the wings of a globally esteemed figure and martyr. Abernathy assured me that there was still much work to be done, even after King and many of the big battles against segregation had been fought and won. The major one being the effort King had made to make poverty a focus of national concern and public policy change.

His words were reassuring. As I walked to the elevator I reflected on his words and the time I spent with him. I felt a pang of regret and a sense that an era had passed. Abernathy who was so much a part of that era, may have been a victim of the inevitable passage of time which had so often left those who had made a movement for change that had accomplished its goals obsolete and an anachronism.

For a time, he reinvented himself by endorsing and participating in various strikes, labor protests, and even drew some heat from blacks for endorsing Ronald Reagan for president in 1980. When Reagan began his assault on affirmative action and federal civil rights protections, he backpedalled and endorsed Reagan's Democratic Presidential opponent, Walter Mondale, in 1984. Abernathy passed in April, 1990. He was 64. He could take solace that he never wavered from King's vision of the need to wage a frontal, aggressive challenge to injustice.

*****

From 1971 to 1973, the *Free Press* continued to be the hub of anti-war and radical protest activity in Los Angeles. When a notable activist came to L.A. to speak at a protest rally or at a college campus protest rally he or she would turn up at the paper's office to meet with Kunkin. More often than not, I'd get the job of interviewing them, and often it would be impromptu. One interview that caught me off guard was the time Kunkin told me that Dr. Benjamin Spock was coming to the *Free Press* in an hour and he wanted a feature on him.

Spock's book the *Common Sense Book of Baby and Child Care*, had been published a quarter century earlier in 1946. It was said to be second only to the Bible in the number of copies sold. But Spock had transitioned from America's wildly popular and most quotable expert on child care and rearing to an impassioned antiwar activist and in the 1972 presidential election, the radical People's Party presidential candidate.

He spoke at dozens of anti-Vietnam war rallies and protests around the country. What sealed his place in the loft of protest history, though, were his indictment, conviction and jail sentence along with four others in 1968 on charges of conspiracy to aid and abet draft resistance. He never served a day of the two year sentence. It was overturned on appeal the next year, 1969.

I sat with Spock in Kunkin's office which he turned over to me on occasion to do in-house interviews with notables. Spock who had rubbed shoulders with the young, long haired, perennially slothful dressed anti-war protestors was dressed in his trademark formal Brooks brothers suit, white shirt and tie. I expected him to be stilted, formal, and correct. He was anything but that. He talked freely about his radical, antiwar activist, and government gadfly conversion. His voice at times rose when he drove home a particular point about how he felt the government had betrayed public trust in waging an illegal and unjust war in Vietnam and promoted unvarnished militarism.

I gingerly asked him whether his view of parenting which had been both reviled and regaled as permissiveness by legions of critics and praised as enlightened parenting for the times by supporters had changed over the years. He gave a terse no, and added only that his views had been grossly distorted about parenting and child rearing. His whole point had always been that children's and later adult's health was enhanced when parents encouraged creative thought and independence in their children. For that he said he made no apology. When I asked whether he wanted to be remembered most for his landmark and near piously regarded book on parenting or his role as antiwar activist, he smiled and said both.

As we walked out of the office, many of the paper's staffers eagerly waited to shake his hand and express their admiration for him. I could see that this suit and tie dressed aging man still possessed a magnetism that could energize those who were two, even three, generations removed from him. I watched him chat with the staffers. They adored him.

He died in 2003. He was 94. Age, though, didn't slow him down. In the 1990s, he was still involved in the editing and discussions of another edition of his parenting book. The passing years also didn't end the controversy about him, his book, and his activism. He claimed in a

1992 interview that book sales were "depressed" during the Vietnam War by his political views. Years later, he said that there were still people who "mistrusted" his book because of his position on social issues. Spock at times may have seemed to be truly a man of another time but he was also a man of these times.

*****

There were very few occasions that I didn't take my tape recorder with me on my travels. I was always on the lookout for an interview, a comment from a personality, or to report on some event. In August 1974, my wife, Yvonne, and my son and daughter, Sikivu and Fanon, and I embarked on my first trip to the South. The end destination was Jackson, Mississippi. I had set up two interviews before leaving. One was with Benny Thompson who had just made history by becoming the first black elected mayor since Reconstruction of Bolton, Mississippi, a small black majority population town, near Jackson. Thompson would later win election in 1993 as the U.S.

Representative for Mississippi's 2nd congressional district. In 2011, he became the ranking member of the Committee on Homeland Security. The other interview was with James Meredith. 12 years earlier, on October 1, 1962, Meredith, an air force veteran, made world news in becoming the first African-American to be admitted the University of Mississippi. This ignited days of bloody riots on the Oxford campus by rabid white segregationists, egged on by saber rattling and defiant threats by Mississippi Governor Ross Barnet and other white state officials. Two were killed in the riots. John F. Kennedy sent hundreds of federal marshals and troops to restore order. The Meredith school admission battle was the second major test of wills since the Little Rock, Arkansas school integration riots in 1957 between the federal government and a Southern state over integration.

In the years since Meredith's admission and the riots, he had somewhat of a wonder lust journey, studying in Africa, then stoking more controversy with his ill-fated walk against racial fear in 1966. This drew global headlines when he was wounded in an ambush attack during the walk. This brought Dr. King and thousands more protestors to the state. One of whom was SNCC Chairman Stokely Carmichael. At one stop along the way, Carmichael shocked the nation with his chant of "Black Power." Meredith then moved to New York and tried to unseat Harlem congressman Adam Clayton Powell, Jr. He ran as a Republican and was squashed in his bid.

He returned to Mississippi and ran for the Senate against another invincible, the ancient Dixiecrat James O. Eastland. Meredith ran again as a Republican. The result was the same. He was crushed. Now 12 years after those momentous days in 1962 at the University of Mississippi, I waited in the coffee shop at a downtown Jackson hotel to talk with the man who had made his place in history. Given the twists and turn in his life after the Mississippi events a decade earlier, I wasn't exactly sure which James Meredith I would be talking too.

The passage of years though hadn't seemed to age him. He still had a youthful cast, was trim, and fit, and walked in with a quick step. He spoke with a slow, thick southern accent. I delved in and immediately asked whether he still reflected on the history making events and the changes that he was at the center of a decade earlier at Ole Miss. He paused for what seemed like minutes. It was almost as if I had caught him off guard with the question, though I knew he had been asked the same question endless times over the years. He said that he hadn't thought much about it, but that there were always reminders of those days in the still lingering overt and subtle vestiges of segregation in the state. As he spoke, I noted that he and I were the only blacks in the coffee shop. I knew that a scant few years earlier neither one of us could have set foot in there.

Meredith talked a lot about his vision and work and his advocacy of building more black businesses as the path to empowerment and his even then controversial embrace of the GOP. He had been roundly lambasted by some black militants as a sell-out and Uncle Tom for it, and had turned into a black conservative. Meredith didn't relent and said that he thought the real future for blacks was in the GOP with their emphasis on business, self-help, and small government. He was convinced this would do more for black advancement than marches, protests and court fights over integration.

I reminded him that this view put him squarely at odds with the major civil rights organizations and black Democrats. He just chuckled and seemed almost pleased that his contrarian stance and embrace of conservative politics had made him a pariah to civil rights leaders. We ended the interview with that. I thanked him for his time, wished him well, and he wished me the best during my stay in the city and the state.

Meredith was a genuine iconic figure who from the moment he stepped on the stage of history with his admission to Ole Miss marched to his own tune. He was emblematic of a grim moment in the civil rights struggle in the early 1960s. The twists and turns in his life in the years after those shattering days could not erase the crucial part he played in breaking down racial barriers. This was the Meredith that history would record as a major figure in the civil rights struggle. No matter how reluctant he was to accept that label. I would remember him for that even as he talked with me about a different vision that he had for the present and the future. Ole Miss for its part had its vision of Meredith. His statue now stands on the campus.

By the 1980s, Meredith's conservatism would not be an anomaly. A host of young, upward mobile, black professionals such as Clarence Thomas would become name players in GOP and conservative political circles then. They would still be the exceptions, though. The 1960s had spawned a black and radical movement that had grown bolder, brasher, and more confrontational. This often included violence. For them, the goal was not change that conformed to the niceties of legality, but radical change. They represented everything that Meredith didn't.

Chapter 2 - The Revolution May Be Televised

In early August, 1968, I had planned to make a return visit to my hometown Chicago. In the eight years since I left the city, much had changed in my old South Side neighborhood. I wanted to make the rounds of my old haunts. African-Americans had moved further to Chicago's South Side into neighborhoods that prior to 1960 had been exclusively white. There were new employment opportunities for black professionals in the major department and retail stores, hotels and corporations based in the Loop downtown.

Parts of the original black areas around 47th St. which in the 1930s and 1940s was the lively center of black Chicago's music scene, were already showing the first signs of gentrification, with younger whites moving into the periphery of that area. I timed my visit to coincide with the start of the Democratic National Convention that was slated for Chicago from August 26 to 28. It would be held at the International Amphitheatre. I had written a couple of articles for the student newspaper at Cal State L.A. and for the mimeographed bulletin churned out by the campus Black Student Union of which I was the vice president. I thought this would be a good opportunity to write a report on the action at the convention. Most of which I knew would be outside the Amphitheatre.

The word had gone out for months before that nearly every radical group in the country would converge on the convention to stage mass protests. The National Mobilization Committee to End the War in Vietnam and the Youth International Party (Yippies) had planned a peace festival to counter the convention. Though President Lyndon Johnson had made the stunning announcement in March, 1968, that he would not seek re-election, he was still a prime target for his escalation of the U.S. war in Vietnam. He was reviled by the left as a war criminal for the bombing, napalming, and mass killing of thousands of Vietnamese. Protesters touted North Vietnamese President Ho Chi Minh as the modern day George Washington. He was elevated to near God like status by them for standing up to the U.S. The universal demand of the protesters was for immediate U.S. withdrawal from Vietnam.

When my wife, Yvonne, and I arrived in Chicago after a three day drive from Los Angeles, we found that the downtown area and areas near the Amphitheatre looked like a battle staging area. The Chicago police backed up by thousands of National Guard troops were out in full force in battle gear on all streets. Chicago Mayor Richard Daley wanted the convention in his city to be a showpiece for the nation. He made no secret that he would use maximum force to prevent any mass disruptions at the convention. The massive show of force by the police virtually guaranteed that there would be confrontations, even violence. The central meeting place for the protest organizers was Grant Park.

When we arrived at the park, it was ringed by police in full battle dress. There were continuous bands and speakers on the main performance stage. There was little doubt that with the tense mood and the heightened presence of police a confrontation was inevitable. It happened quickly. Club swinging police moved in on the crowd, pushing, shoving and pummeling many who attempted to flee in the panic.

In the midst of the chaos, an eerie sound came from the stage. Renowned counter culture poet Allen Ginsberg sat lotus like in the middle of the stage and chanted the Buddhist OM OM OM His eyes were tightly closed as he continued to chant amidst the swirling tear gas and the bone crunching sounds of nightsticks hitting flesh. It was bedlam with police frantically chasing demonstrators up and down the adjacent streets and into the downtown area near the main hotels where the convention delegates were staying. Ginsberg, though, was unfazed. Even as we managed to make our way out of the park, I could still hear his OMs.

By then things had deteriorated into a tragic passion play. Protest leaders would try to mount a mass march and police would quickly move in to attack. The whole scene had degenerated into a chaotic jumble of arrests, violence, and near anarchy. We could not get back to our car which was parked next to the park and in the center of the melee. We ducked, dodged and maneuvered our way around barricades to an El station. The next day we took the El back to the park. There were still squads of police there. We cautiously eased our way to our car taking frequent wary glances at the police.

The protest drew global attention and was a supreme embarrassment to a Democratic Party that was already under intense political siege. It was torn by divisions within from an insurgent anti-war faction led by Minnesota Senator Eugene McCarthy, and Robert F. Kennedy who had declared his candidacy, and the thinly disguised race driven breakaway insurgency by Alabama Governor George Wallace. The party's disarray could only work to the advantage of GOP Presidential candidate Richard Nixon. He would play hard on the Democrat's woes and steal a page from Wallace by lambasting the Democrats for supposedly creating the climate of permissiveness, anarchy, and law breaking. Johnson's designated replacement candidate, Vice President Hubert Humphrey, the party's eventual presidential nominee was irreparably hurt by the massive disruptions and disorder at the convention.

*****

The violence at the Democratic convention that I had witnessed in the streets was just the start of my being an on the scene witness to other violent confrontations between police and protestors. Much of that violence then squarely centered on the clash between the Black Panther Party and the police on one side, and between the Panthers and other black organizations on the other.

I had just published my first article in the New York based *Guardian* newspaper in 1969. It carried a range of articles and think pieces by the leading progressive and black activist writers, intellectuals and scholars of the day. The piece I wrote was a lengthy examination of the deep splits that had developed between those that adhered to an African based, cultural or Pan Africanist view and those who called themselves radical black nationalists. They generally advocated for militant confrontation with the police and armed self-defense. This conflict would later explode into open warfare between the Black Panther Party and the Black Nationalist organization, US, founded by Maulana Karenga in Los Angeles.

The clash came to a horrific head in a wild shoot out on the UCLA campus in January 1969. It resulted in the slaying of two Panthers, John Huggins and Alprentice Bunchy Carter, at UCLA by US members. Their deaths touched a personal nerve with me. A year earlier, Carter and Huggins had spoken at one of our Black Student Union meetings at Cal State L.A. I, and other students, cringed as Carter ripped into us for not being militant enough. Shortly after that, I attended a panel discussion at UCLA in which Ericka Huggins, John's wife, was a panelist. Huggins was there. He sat quietly in the rear during the panel discussion. I immediately thought about his quiet, unassuming, presence at that earlier discussion.

The year 1969 that began with Huggins murder, ended with yet another violent encounter involving the Panthers. I had just started work as a social worker in Watts with the L.A. County Department of Social Services. The morning of November 28, 1969 a co-worker rushed excitedly into the office and said to check out the news. There was a gun battle raging between the Panthers and the LAPD, he said, at the Panther office on Central Avenue. It was located two miles away from my office. I jumped in the car and drove to the scene. There was a massive crowd outside the ramshackle building on 41st and Central Ave. This was the headquarters of the L.A. Black Panthers. Every time a shot went up from the Panther office there was a loud cheer from the predominantly black crowd. In between the chaos, several individuals were making a frantic effort to negotiate a cease fire. One of them was then California state senator Mervyn Dymally. He would later make history as the modern era's first black lieutenant governor of California, and as a congressman.

Dymally looked disheveled, and thoroughly spent, as he ran from one police official to another trying to get their attention. He was having little luck. The LAPD was in full attack mode and poured a barrage of gunfire and tear gas into the building. This was clearly a search and destroy mission. The police and the FBI had then declared the Panthers the number one domestic threat. They were targeted for extinction. The battle didn't last long. As the Panthers stumbled out of the building with their arms raised in surrender, I watched dozens of officers rush at them in swarms, shoving them to the ground and clamping shackles on them. The crowd jeered and cursed the police even louder.

The confrontation refocused attention on the continuing legal battle of Black Panther founder Huey Newton. He had been convicted the year before for the October, 1967 murder of Oakland police officer John Frey. His trial and conviction on voluntary manslaughter and his sentence of 2 to 15 years made Newton a *cause celebre* among many blacks and radical activists throughout the country. The poster of him seated in a wicker chair holding a spear and gun and in full Panther regalia, black beret and black leather jacket, was plastered on walls and buildings in dozens of cities. The legal maneuvering by famed leftist attorney Charles Garry to keep Newton off death row and get a conviction on lesser charges had in itself become the subject of much debate and massive press attention. The Panthers had raised thousands of dollars for his defense. Garry prevailed. The conviction was overturned on appeal two years later and in two subsequent trials the juries hung and the case against Newton was dropped.

Four years after the murder of Frey, things had changed. Newton had stirred controversy of a different sort when he moved into an exclusive pent house complex overlooking the chic Lake Merritt neighborhood in Oakland. More than a few questioned the propriety of the man who had become the emblem of black radical militancy, and the head of an organization that for four years had called for revolution, and now lived in palatial splendor. Newton's retort was that the penthouse arrangement was necessary solely for security reasons, presumably because of death threats that he had received. In any case, I had travelled to Oakland specifically to interview him for the *Free Press*. I would do the interview with him at his penthouse apartment. I exited the elevator on the top floor and was immediately met, questioned and searched by his heavy set menacing, unsmiling bodyguard who walked me into the apartment. A relaxed Newton sat on a love seat in a silk smoking jacket. He greeted me with a broad smile, and a sheepish grin. I gazed out the large window at the panoramic view of Oakland and the San Francisco bay that was visible behind him.

The interview was less an interview than a lengthy, rambling monologue by Newton on the Panther history, his new found interest in and push for blacks to vote, and to run candidates for office. Newton also talked a lot about his growing embrace of black capitalism as a panacea for black empowerment. There was no talk of guns, denunciations of the police, or any mention of revolutionary international figures that had marked the Panthers in 1969. This was a new workmanlike and business oriented Newton. It seemed a total repudiation of the Panther's gun toting, slogan shouting radical days, and confrontations with the police.

Newton had been harshly denounced by radical activists and break off elements of the Panthers. The seed of that split, though, had emerged with Newton's highly publicized feud with Eldridge Cleaver in 1971 after Cleaver was expelled from the party over his bellicose push for urban guerrilla attacks on the police by then from exile in Algeria. This spawned a bitter round of internal warfare, sometimes violent between the Cleaver and Newton factions. It resulted in the almost comic series of expulsions, most notably of Cleaver, and his subsequent flight from the country and asylum in Cuba and Algeria.

There were also the requisite denunciations of other top Panthers such as Elmer Geronimo Pratt who sided with the Cleaver faction. The two factions would engage in a caustic feud that at times was marked by gunfire for two years.

*****

Yet, as Newton talked about his emphasis on electoral politics and business, the image of Cleaver stayed in my mind. Cleaver's odyssey from rapist, to celebrated prison writer, to internationally acclaimed author, with his wildly successful, *Soul on Ice* published in 1968 had made him an instant movement celebrity. His rough-hewn, profane violence laced talks, and street thug veneer, made him an alluring object of fascination. I saw it on full display twice. The first time was when he was drafted to be the Peace and Freedom Party's presidential candidate in 1968. One of his "campaign" stops was at L.A.'s Griffith Park. The occasion was an anti-Vietnam war protest rally there. I watched as Cleaver strolled through the crowd as if he was Moses parting the red Sea. He was mobbed, touched and fawned as if he was a top rock star.

Cleaver was anything but the gracious recipient of their adoration. He spat out a rough stream of MFs and assorted expletives interspersed with rants against the "pigs" and denounced what he called "boot licking Negro leaders," and the rotten capitalist system. He pretty much repeated this expletive laced diatribe when he took the microphone. He didn't speak for long and as quickly as he appeared he was whisked away by a phalanx of black leather jacketed Panther escorts.

He held a perverse fascination for me as well. I was enthralled by his profane and irreverent gutter, pugnacious, and thumb his nose at conventions demeanor. He was in many ways an anomaly among what was then a sea of anomalies that characterized many of the fringe characters in radical organizations at that time. Cleaver's contempt for his audience was again on full display when he was the featured speaker at Los Angeles Trade Tech College in the fall of 1968. The auditorium was packed and there was a buzz of anticipation at how Cleaver would come off at a community college.

Cleaver wasted no time launching into his standard rip of the police, conservative blacks, and movement charlatans. Then he took a turn that even by his ribald standards sent a shock through the audience. He paused and shouted out that the Panther's believed that the role of women in the movement was prone. There was an audible gasp. Cleaver paused again seemingly to let the shock sink in. He said the only power that women had was sexual power. (He actually used a pejorative for sex that starts with "P").

That did it. First one, then three, and then other women stormed out of the auditorium. The catcalls and boos rained down. Cleaver was oblivious to them and continued with his graphic diatribe about the demeaning and subservient role of women. As I watched this embarrassing spectacle unfold, I wondered just how had Cleaver managed to drape himself with the mantle of a black revolutionary, and therefore supposedly a progressive. The truth was that once the façade of him being an enlightened figure was stripped away Cleaver was still the same Cleaver who bragged in his book about his delight in his rapes. In that moment, I, and the audience, did not see and hear, a black radical, but a woman hating, rapist, and ex-convict.

The word quickly got out that if you invite Cleaver to a campus get ready to hear women demeaned and denigrated. This was a Cleaver that many campuses quickly hung the not wanted sign up for. By then he had become fugitive Cleaver when he jumped bail following his arrest on charges of attempting to murder police officers in an Oakland gun battle. His flight to avoid being dumped back in prison for a parole violation was the beginning of his strange odyssey from Cuba to Algeria and China. In 1975, he returned and declared that he was a born again Christian. He died in May 1998. He was 62.

*****

Listening to Newton that warm spring afternoon at his apartment wax about his newfound vision of black economic empowerment, I thought about the perverse, warped, but fascinating, revolutionary odyssey of Newton's nemesis, Cleaver. When I heard of his death in May, 1998, it conjured up again that scene at Trade Tech of the women who fled in horror at his denigration of them.

Newton did not make mention of the feud with Cleaver and the accompanying strife it engendered. By then Cleaver was a distant memory. His sole focus now was on the Panther's new bid for mainstream respectability. This was not the last time I'd hear Newton espouse his message of entrepreneurship and electoral politics. A year later in April 1972, he spoke to the National Association of Black Manufacturers, a black business and trade group, at the Hacienda Hotel near the Los Angeles airport in El Segundo, California. I covered the speech. He told the small assembly of black entrepreneurs and business professionals that the Panthers were out to "transform" the system. He left no doubt what that meant to him. He said that he was now out "to get as much money as possible." After all he added with a wry smile, "You can't build a liberation movement without it." Newton's full throated endorsement of black capitalism as the path to black empowerment was a huge hit with the gathering. They loudly applauded.

As I listened to his speech, I thought about the interview I did with him months earlier at his Penthouse apartment and how different things had turned out with an organization, and its leader, who once espoused revolution and now embraced the very antithesis of that. By the mid-1970s, the Panthers were defunct and Newton had fled to Havana where he was offered asylum after being charged with murder in a street altercation. He returned in 1977, got a Ph.D., and stayed largely out of public view for the next decade. However, violence once again found him when in yet another street altercation in 1989, he was shot and killed. Supposedly the last words he uttered were "You can kill my body, and you can take my life but you can never kill my soul. My soul will live forever!" He was 47.

Newton's death ironically by violence marked the passing of an era when a black organization had the temerity to pick up guns, and frontally challenge the armed might of the American state. It was bold, brash, outrageous, and at times theatrical, but whatever criticisms could be made of the Panthers violent rhetoric, adventurism, and fool hardiness, many blacks hailed them for their stand. Newton deserved some credit for that.

*****

Newton and the Panthers for a time had energized black activists in Los Angeles as in few other cities. The pinnacle of this was the event on the afternoon of February 18, 1968 at the L.A. Sports Arena. The arena was the scene for a giant Birthday Celebration for Newton. It brought the leading lights in the black radical and black power movement together. These individuals then had become top targets of the FBI's COINTELPRO program. That was a covert and patently illegal program concocted by FBI Director J. Edgar Hoover to divide, disrupt, and dismember black radical organizations by planting a network of agents, provocateurs, poison pen letters, and staging coordinated attacks and raids on Panther offices with local police departments in several cities.

The Newton Birthday tribute rally was also billed as a unity rally. A formal announcement would be made there that the Black Panthers and the Student Nonviolent Coordinating Committee would merge and that SNCC leaders Rap Brown, James Forman, and Carmichael (soon to become Kwame Toure) would become Panther ministers. I and a few other BSU members were ecstatic when the word went out that the organizers needed volunteers to act as monitors at the arena. We readily agreed. I saw it as a chance of a lifetime to see and hear the most prominent black radical leaders in one place at one time. We got there early and were told to walk the aisles and keep a look out for any disturbances. The crowd was huge and there was no hint of any trouble.

Many there actually believed that the black revolution was on the cusp of becoming a reality. This hope would be sorely dashed with the ensuing expulsions, splits, and gunfire that in a few short months would ensue between rival black radical groups. All of which was generously helped along by the relentless, clandestine assault by the FBI aimed at destroying the black radical movement and those that made the movement.

SNCC's executive secretary, James Forman, kicked things off. He was the prime initiator of the widely publicized "unity" talks with the Panther leaders. He skipped the niceties and menacingly warned of "retribution" if any black leaders were killed by the police or FBI. He meant Carmichael, himself and Newton, and Brown. Forman was careful not to spell out exactly what "retribution" meant.

He was followed by Reies Tijerina who had made national news the year before in 1967 when he and his band of land grant protestors was arrested and charged with multiple counts of kidnapping and armed assault after a massive manhunt in New Mexico. They had attempted an armed takeover of a courthouse. Tijerina was flanked by a contingent of Brown Berets in a display of black-brown unity. This was rapidly becoming the watch word in the radical movement. Tijerina gave a fiery talk scoring the government for "stealing" the land from the nation's indigenous peoples.

After what seemed like endless speeches and posturing, Carmichael took the stage. He shouted that he would be gleeful if the country burned to the ground, and warned that "fifteen honkies" would die if

Newton were harmed. This was standard talk among Panthers. Other than the FBI and nervous police officials, few really believed it was anything but bellicose rhetoric. I had heard that talk enough to take it for what it was. I was far more interested in hearing Carmichael talk about his recent travels to a number of African and Asian countries and how he was received by their foreign radical leaders. He said virtually nothing about that. I was deflated at this glaring omission. The rally quietly ended. I left the Sports Arena with the uneasy feeling that the rally was little more than a giant feel good session; and now what?

Carmichael did not leave L.A. after the rally. I still wanted to hear his "report" on his trip and what it meant for blacks here. I got another chance hopefully to hear him talk about that experience when I learned he would speak to a small gathering at the offices of the Black Congress on Broadway in South L.A. Again, I was disappointed. He pretty much followed the same script as his speech at the Sports Arena and said almost nothing about his travels. After he spoke, I hovered on the sidewalk outside the building waiting for a chance to ask him about his trip. As he exited, and stood for a moment chatting with admirers, I timidly approached and asked him if he had met Mao. Carmichael grinned and recited a cryptic quote from Mao's *Red Book* then a hot ticket item among radicals, "support what the enemy opposes and oppose what the enemy supports."

This was about as close as I got to learning from him about what the leaders in China that I was told he met with had to say about the Panthers, SNCC, the Black Power and black consciousness movement in this country. I wanted to know if they felt any real kinship with those struggles. The unity that the Panthers and SNCC and other radicals promised didn't last long. Cleaver was in exile. SNCC had dissolved. The Panthers were divided and under assault from police and state agencies and from other competing black organizations. The dangerous fantasies of making a violent revolution in the U.S. would soon give way in the early 1970s to an emphasis on black business, electing more blacks to office, and grabbing jobs in corporations, and at universities. Carmichael would become Kwame Toure, and settle in Guinea, and become a kind of elder statesman for Pan Africanism.

He died in 1998. He was 57. Carmichael would be known for his unrelenting condemnation of racism and capitalism and his coining of the term black power. Perhaps his greatest contribution, though, was the focus he put on what would be called "institutional racism." This is the structural inequality built into race relations in America. However, history remembers him. I gave him great credit for awakening many young blacks to the importance of black political empowerment. That included me. That was the message I took away from the encounters I had with him.

Chapter 3
Africans Unite

Chapter 3 - Africans Unite!

In the early 1970s, Pan-Africanism became increasingly more attractive for many black activists. It had roots that reached back more than a century and a half. The Wikipedia textbook definition of Pan Africanism is "an ideology and movement that encourages the solidarity of Africans worldwide. It is based on the belief that unity is vital to economic, social, and political progress and aims to "unify and uplift" people of African descent." This broad, sweeping, and very general definition of Pan-Africanism was subject to wide interpretation depending on whose lips the words came out of it.

I would discover this time and again after I was accepted as part of the inaugural class at the newly established Africana Studies and Research Center at Cornell University in September 1970. The center was borne out of the stunning, headline grabbing takeover and occupation on April 19, 1969, by 80 members of Cornell's Afro-American Society during a parents' weekend of the student union building at Willard Straight Hall in protest of racial tensions. They also demanded greater support for a black studies program. The picture of students emerging after the prolonged stand -off waving, smiling, with clenched fists in the air and brandishing guns was captured globally in newspapers. It rammed home the fears and paranoia in many Americans that there was something threatening, menacing and sinister afoot with the black movement, and among blacks. The administration, under intense pressure and duress from the black students, caved in to their demand for a black studies center.

I felt part of a unique, even pioneering experiment in education in being accepted in the program at the center. This was the first significant step taken by a major university toward putting its academic body and resources into a potentially degree granting center for black students. The overriding philosophy of the center's administration and faculty was that it would be an explicitly Afrocentric program. To insure that there was a constant parade of guest lecturers, and speakers on history, and politics. The study of African history was stressed.

The biggest name speaker that first year was Shirley Graham DuBois, the wife of the black scholar and activist W.E.B. DuBois. Her visit took on even more importance for me when the center's director James Turner asked me to be part of the official student greeting committee for her. Part of our duties was to pick her up at the airport and act as her escort and help mates during her stay at Cornell.

Graham Dubois was the living link to the man who was one of the founders of the Niagara Movement and later the NAACP in 1909. For nearly a half century, from the latter part of the 19th Century to the first decades of the 20th Century, DuBois was the reigning academic, intellectual, activist, scholar, and writer in black America.

Graham DuBois's trip to the center was the first time she had been back in the country since moving to Ghana in 1961. She and DuBois had made their home there at the personal invitation of Ghanaian President Kwame Nkrumah whose books on Pan Africanism and African liberation had made him into a widely quoted folk hero among black activists in America. In Ghana, DuBois started work on compiling a major work, the *Encyclopedia Africana*, that would chronicle the achievement and works of black writers, scholars, and historical figures. Following DuBois death in 1963, and a coup in 1967 that toppled Nkrumah, she moved to Cairo, Egypt.

Graham Dubois, though she had just turned 75, was a ball of energy and dynamism. In the car she was witty, feisty, and talked non-stop. She sounded like a cross between a cheer leader and raconteur. She peppered us with anecdotes about the DuBois and life in Ghana. She constantly exhorted us to fight, fight and continue to fight for justice here. Graham Dubois saw racial gains as grossly incomplete. She was convinced that the energy and drive of students here was the key to progress. She was scathing in her denunciation of established black organizations such as the NAACP. DuBois's very pronounced leftist leaning got him in hot water with fearful NAACP officials in the late 1940s. The McCarthy anti-communist hysteria was on the rise in the U.S at the time and any association with DuBois was a liability. She felt the NAACP had betrayed DuBois by unceremoniously urging his resignation because of his views in 1948.

DuBois was indicted and tried for his association with an alleged Communist front group in 1950. Though the case was dropped, he was denied a passport for eight years. An aging and embittered DuBois joined the Communist Party in 1961. This was his final defiant act at his treatment by a country in which he had been one the nativist of native sons and had made profound contributions to the then burgeoning civil rights movement in the early decades of the 20th

Century. When his passport was reinstated, he and Graham DuBois renounced their American citizenship and moved to Ghana.

Graham DuBois stayed at Cornell for two days. She addressed several classes and concluded with an open lecture. She took more barbs and jabs at the civil rights leaders, praised progressive African leaders, especially Nkrumah, and talked about life with DuBois. She was animated, funny, and focused. As I listened, I realized that this remarkable woman had been far more than the wife of W.E.B. DuBois. She was an important scholar and activist in her own right and combined the same unique blend of scholarship and activism that made her husband an acclaimed historical figure. She signed her recently published memoir on W.E.B. DuBois in the car on the way back to airport. She again exhorted us to keep struggling for what we believed was right. She died in March 1977. She was 80.

*****

Graham DuBois's visit along with that of other speakers was one of many highs of my year at Cornell. Every class was like an advanced seminar on some aspect of African and African-American history, culture, politics, economics, and social studies. Often a noted guest lecturer would pop in. The administration took great care to insure that students did not falter in their course work. They assigned each student a faculty mentor. Mine was John Henrik Clarke. Clarke was a walking history. His voluminous writings, speeches and lectures were in many libraries and his books were used in courses at major universities.

Clarke lived in his three story Brownstone in Harlem since the early 1930s. It had become a landmark. Many of the major figures of the Harlem Renaissance, Langston Hughes, Countee Cullen, and A. Phillip Randolph had visited Clarke at his home. Every room was stacked with books from the floor to the ceiling. They ranged over a broad number of topics. Clarke was a man of unlimited intellectual interest.

It didn't take long for our relationship to blossom into one of unbridled mutual respect and admiration. I had one big advantage over the other students. I was a published author. In 1970, my first book the *Myth of Black Capitalism* was published by *Monthly Review Press*, a popular left publishing house in New York City. Copies of the book were in the center's library. This gave me an elevated status that the other professors and Clarke recognized. I was both a student and a potential resource for the center.

Clarke saw me the same way. On several weekends when I hitched a ride to New York City with students that lived in the city, I stayed at Clarke's home. I sat for hours with him listening as he ranged over many topics. He was a master conversationalist. There was always that earthy, caring, and solicitous aspect to him. It came through in the way that he dealt with people

Clarke was a man who you didn't just respect as a paramount scholar and writer, but also as a genuine caring person. In the spring, 1971, Clarke had announced that he would pitch *Beacon Press*, a Boston based, liberal Unitarian church founded publisher, to publish my thesis. I had chosen as my subject the study of the life of Henry Highland Garnet, who along with black abolitionist Frederick Douglass, was considered a preeminent figure in the pre-Civil War anti-slavery movement. Garnet also was an early advocate of black consciousness. He was also a prominent minister, writer, and speaker. His speech at an anti-slavery convention in Buffalo, New York in 1843 with its call to rebellion had been widely quoted and cited for decades as a clarion call against racial injustice. My goal was to restore Garnet's place as a seminal early advocate of civil rights and black nationalism.

Beacon Press was in the process of then publishing a series of books on black historical figures and topics. Clarke was as good as his word and I got a contract for the book. I devoted weeks to compiling original source materials that included letters, articles, newspaper clippings, speeches, sermons, and an early biographical sketch of Garnet. In 1972, *Let Your Motto be Resistance*, Garnet's biography, was published. By then I had left Cornell and returned to L.A. and had started work at the *Free Press*. The first copy of the book that I received I autographed and sent to Clarke. In the following years, we occasionally talked by phone and we maintained a spotty correspondence. Clarke's health by then had deteriorated badly. He had gone blind. Yet there was never a hint of despair or self-pity when we talked. He maintained an active speaking and lecturing schedule. It seemed that he always had a new book in preparation.

There was a bitter sweet moment in 1998 on my visit to New York. As always when in the city I would telephone him or travel to Harlem to visit. I got word that Clarke had now moved into an apartment with his wife, in upper Harlem, and that his health had taken a turn for the worse. Barbara, my second wife, and I, immediately jumped on the subway to his residence.

I was shocked at his weight loss and his pronounced aging. Yet, he had not lost any of his verbosity. He reminisced about figures he had known, African issues and politics, and the importance of preserving our history. We embraced warmly. I knew it would be our last embrace.

Clarke passed away in July 1998. He was 83. The tributes on him were effusive. All acknowledged the profound contribution he made to the scholarly study and promotion of African history and Pan Africanist studies. No words could describe the joy I felt when some years later Clarke's Brownstone was declared a historic monument and the street it was on was christened John Henrik Clarke Square. The Africana Studies Center established the John Henrik Clarke Africana Library. He made the African ancestors that he revered in his speeches, lectures, writings, and talks with me and thousands of others during his profound and illustrious life proud.

The late 1960s and 1970s spawned a flowering of in your face black consciousness in the music and arts world. The list of musicians, writers and actors and actresses that paid nods to that in their works was growing longer. I was in the perfect spot to see, hear, and in many cases talk to some of the best and brightest names in their fields at the *Free Press* and KPFK. I made the most of that opportunity.

Chapter 4
A Cultural Revolution

Chapter 4 - A Cultural Revolution

All the students at Holy Cross, the Catholic elementary school I attended on Chicago's South Side, were required every Christmas to sell boxes of Christmas cards. This was one of the many ways the school raised funds. It was Christmas, 1958, and I was 12. The student that sold the most boxes would get a prize usually a ribbon, or a certificate. It was a blustery day when I made the rounds from door to door a couple of blocks from my house. I hadn't had much luck so far in getting a sale. My luck changed though in a way I had not expected when I knocked on a door three blocks from my house. The large woman that opened the door at first gave me a quizzical look, and asked if she could help me.

I stammered that I was selling Christmas cards for my school and would she like to buy a box. My stammer became more pronounced when I recognized the woman who was standing in front of me. It was Mahalia Jackson. I had heard the name many times from my parents who often played a 78 recording of Jackson's *Take My Hand, Precious Lord*. My father who was a deacon at the nearby Woodlawn African Methodist Episcopal Church played this endlessly and would softly hum the melody along with it.

I knew that she lived somewhere in the neighborhood. Jackson took pride in living in our South Side neighborhood and even when she had the opportunity to live elsewhere she made it clear that she preferred to live in the all black part of Chicago's South Side. The part we lived in.

It was no mean feat for her to get that house. Her international acclaim meant little to her white neighbors. They launched a prolonged campaign to get her out of the neighborhood that culminated with shots fired at her window. The whites soon stampeded from the neighborhood. What was once an exclusively white neighborhood on Chicago's South Side within a year had flipped into a nearly all black neighborhood by the time we moved there in 1957. Jackson stayed put.

She quickly sized me up and without any hesitation said I'll take the box. I thought she meant one box. As I reached for one, she abruptly said, no I meant the whole box. The box contained about a dozen small boxes of Christmas cards. I was speechless. She quickly handed me a ten dollar bill, took the box, wished me a merry Christmas and closed the door. I stood there for a long moment on her front porch clutching the ten dollar bill, which to me was a small fortune. Her gesture was a simple gesture of heartfelt kindness to a kid whose only thought was selling a couple of boxes of Christmas cards and being done with the chore. Jackson confirmed what many would repeatedly say about her that she had a heart as big as gold. She loved her God, her music and her people and would do anything for them. Jackson had earned a coveted place as the "Queen of Gospel" and even then had begun what would become a long and fruitful working relationship with Dr. King.

Her appearances at the SCLC conventions and fundraising efforts on behalf of the organization gave it a tremendous boost. Jackson was the living embodiment of the gospel tradition that has been the staple of black churches and a source of powerful spiritual uplift and comfort for many blacks through the decades of slavery and Jim Crow segregation. Jackson in addition to being hailed as the gospel queen had attained a revered place in the burgeoning civil rights movement. She died in January, 1972, in Chicago. She was 60.

Whenever I hear Jackson's immortalized classic, *He's Got the Whole World in his Hand* and *Amazing Grace*, I don't think of the Mahalia Jackson of international acclaim and adulation. I think of the big hearted woman who smiled down on a young boy with boxes of Christmas cards that stood in the cold on her front porch. She offered him a kind gesture that could never be forgotten.

*****

My first job after graduating from Dorsey High School in Los Angeles was a summer job as an usher at the famed Hollywood Bowl. It was a dream job. I got to see many of the leading musical acts of the day that were booked into the bowl. However, the concert the night of August 23, 1964 would be different. All the ushers were told to stay as close to the stage as possible and to stay on guard for a rush from the crowd. We were told that the group that was booked into the bowl might ignite delirium among the crowd.

This put it mildly. The instant *the Beatles* sprinted on to the stage there was mass hysteria. It was all I and the other ushers could do to keep the crowd from mobbing the stage. When they launched into the number that had made them world renowned, *I want to hold your hand,* it was sheer bedlam. The shrieks from the mostly 16 and 17 year old girls were deafening. The Beatles quickly followed that with *Twist and Shout, You Can't Do That, Can't Buy Me Love, If I Fell,* and *A Hard Day's Night.* They could barely be heard over the screams and shouts of the crowd. I stared as if in a trance at the stage that these four long haired young white performers from Britain in their tight squarish looking suits could create such hysteria in so many people. I knew that whoever they were, they were here to stay and something new, dynamic and original had burst on the American musical and cultural scene. The British wave that hit Los Angeles that August night in 1964 ushered in a new era and I was there to see it.

I had no inkling that one of the young men I watched on stage that night could ever have a tragic end. John Lennon had created a furor in the U.S. a year after the Beatles Bowl appearance when he said the group was more popular than Jesus. He didn't endear himself to conservatives as he moved steadily left and became an outspoken anti-war activist and wrote songs such as *Power to the People* that were unabashed protest songs.

A few years after their Bowl appearance, the Beatles as a group were no more. But Lennon continued to compose, perform, and occasionally stoke controversy. The tragedy caught up to him in December, 1980 when he was shot dead outside of his New York City apartment building. He was 40. I noted that Lennon's birthday was October 9, the day after mine. I felt we had lost a first rate superb, thinker, activist, and musician. To me, though, he was still a Beatle.

In the fall of 1973 I began a weekly hour long jazz and arts show on KPFK radio. It was the standard mix of music and interviews with jazz, and R&B notables who were performing in L.A. Since this was one of the few jazz and R&B music and talk shows on the FM dial at the time in L.A., I got many requests from record company publicists to interview their artists. One of the first to come to the station was a short, light complexioned, boyish looking singer in town on tour from Jamaica. Unlike many of the others I had never heard of him and I was not familiar with his music. I hadn't really listened to it. The interview as it turned out was much more than I had bargained for. Bob Marley and his group the Wailers had just started their first American tour. They had played at concerts in Boston, and New York in July. And now in October they were in Los Angeles for a recording session at Capitol Records studios in Hollywood.

During the half hour interview, Marley did not utter one line about anything musical. He talked rapid fire, in his thick Jamaican accent that was barely intelligible to me about his belief in and devotion to Rastafarianism. He hailed Haile Selassie and the 1920s Black Nationalist leader Marcus Garvey as his heroes. Much of this was foreign to me. I listened enthralled at his discourse, and was mesmerized by his tangle of flowing twisted coarse hair. When the show ended, Marley continued talking about and praising Rastafarianism. This answer that he gave to an interviewer later about Rastafarianism was virtually a carbon of how he described his belief in the half hour he was in studio with me, "Now, the Bible seh so, Babylon newspaper seh so, and I and I the children seh so. Yunno? So I don't see how much more reveal our people want. Wha' dem want? a white God, well God come black. True true."

He prophesized that one day the movement would go global and have a profound impact on tens of thousands. He was right. In the years since his untimely passing at age 36 in May, 1981, numerous persons have asked me about that day in the studio with Marley, what he was like and what it felt like to interview him. For a time on February 6, his birthday, which is celebrated internationally as Bob Marley day complete with monster Reggae concerts, I would get a request from a radio station in Jamaica to talk about Marley and what had come to be called "the interview." Marley was the first musician that I had ever interviewed that did not utter a word about his music but his spiritual beliefs. Music might have been his message, but religion was his life. Even though I listened often and became a devotee of Marley's music, it was his passionate expression of his beliefs that endeared him to me.

*****

I positioned the show as a go to show for R&B and jazz artists on tour in L.A. In one year I had the Jazz Crusaders, Stanley Turentine, Yuseff Lateef, Isaac Hayes, Freddie Hubbard, Les McCann, Eddie Harris, to name a few in studio. I was especially intrigued listening to Barry White when he guested on my show in July, 1974 talk of his great love of classical music and how he blended this into his unique orchestral arrangements with the *Love Unlimited Orchestra*. I let White know that I would be front and center in the audience the first night of his five day concert at the L.A. Sports Arena. His orchestra looked exactly like a classical musical symphonic orchestra in the way the instrument sections were arranged on stage and dressed in their classical music hall formal attire. White had created a matchless and imaginative blend of the classics and pop tunes. His big, deep, and sensual bass delivery vocals enhanced his special musical sound.

White died in July, 2003. He was 58. As a classical music lover, I felt I was almost at a classical music concert every time I heard White's blend of strings and brass to pop rhythms. It was no accident he was called the maestro. He was a classicist in a pop artist's clothing. This set a new standard in the pop sound that made White unforgettable.

There was hardly a week during the next five years that I was not at some concert, play, or club either doing an interview with one of the performers or a review of their act. One club I was a fixture at was the Ash Grove near Hollywood. It was the Holy Grail for blues performers coming to L.A. then. Anybody who was anybody in the blues world appeared at the Grove. I'd usually go backstage during intermission and get a few minutes of comment from the performers in between their sets. That's how I met and talked with Lightnin' Hopkins, John Lee Hooker, Big Mama Thornton, Albert King, and Big Mabel. They were gracious and extremely generous with their time with me. They gave me grounding not only in their musical styles and performance but also the sense of the pain, suffering, joy and pleasure that the blues conveyed from the soul of the black experience in America.

The blues had long since transcended that experience. It had a sledgehammer impact on a generation of white artists. Elvis Presley. The Animals, Fleetwood Mac, John Mayall & the Bluesbreakers, The Rolling Stones, The Yardbirds, Cream and Irish musician Rory Gallagher had recorded and performed classic blues songs at one time or another. They had cashed in big on the songs, while the originators still received peanuts, if that, for their songs. When I brought this up with Lightnin' Hopkins, he just shrugged and said that he was happy that blues music had found a wider audience.

*****

I owe Richie Havens a profound debt of gratitude. In the late 1960s, when I thought of folk music, I thought of a white kid strumming a guitar and singing country music mixed with some hippie or antiwar lyrics. It was music that had no appeal to my Motown, rhythm and blues and jazz loving ears. There was simply nothing in the least bit "soulful," let alone black, I thought, to folk music.

Havens showed me how wrong I was. I heard him in 1971 at the Ash Grove in Los Angeles two years after his breakout appearance in 1969 at the Woodstock Festival.

Havens was on the bill with a couple of other blues artists. When he came on stage with his strum guitar and the MC billed him as one of the country's most talented folk singers, I groaned. It took exactly one number for that to change. I was spellbound by his raw, pointed, yet lilting voice, and the fury and the passion with which he crushed number after number.

What truly captivated me, beyond the brilliance of his musical artistry, was that this was a black man who could take a musical genre I wrongly assumed was a "white thing" and turn it into a rollicking, soulful experience. Havens did not just defy the stereotype that I had of folk music and musicians, he shattered it.

In addition, this was the late 1960s, and one felt the power and the militant spirit of the civil rights and peace movement in his music.

After that night, I became a fervent devotee of Havens. I made sure to stock my album collection with his music. I badly wanted to interview him the times that he would play in L.A. There was always some assignment that I had that conflicted with arranging a time and place for the interview. It was a missed opportunity that I regretted.

It was no surprise when Havens held the tens of thousands at Woodstock in rapt attention, and later the multitudes that saw his spell binding performance in the Woodstock film.

The concert promoters had beseeched him to stay on stage longer to fill up time. The audience heard and saw a grimacing, pounding, relentless Havens wailing out what would become his signature work, "Freedom." This was a work that was more or less improvised from the ancient black standard "Motherless Child." This sealed Havens name and fame forever.

In truth, Havens had been his own musical man and trend setter for many years. From the moment he left Brooklyn in the early 1960s and took up residence in Greenwich Village, he had taken an intense interest in folk music and as he reminisced later "the poetry and the song of the Beatnik days of the 1950s." His musical journey quickly brought him to the folk and music guru of the day, Bob Dylan. Havens was managed by Dylan's manager, and contributed the cover song to Dylan's "Just Like a Woman." At the time of his Woodstock appearance he had released five albums.

The next two decades, the ubiquitous Havens cut albums and TV commercials, was a constant on the touring circuit, and even found time to dabble in films and TV, and play a lead part in a staged production of "Othello." By the 1990s, Havens had truly become America's long-standing universal ambassador for folk music and world peace. He capped this in the 1990s with a performance at Bill Clinton's first inauguration in 1993 and later a featured performance at the Tibetan Freedom Concert.

Havens backed up his musical and peace advocacy by establishing a foundation to promote environmental causes and education among inner-city youth. It wasn't just his non-stop advocacy of folk music and peace that made him a standout figure; Havens was just as determined to devote his time and talent to a variety of causes and charities. If there was a peace or civil rights movement fund raiser that needed a headline artist, more often than not Havens would be the one. He truly believed that his music and art should be of, by, and for the people.

Fittingly, one of his last concerts before he announced he would end touring after 45 years was a benefit concert in 2009 for the legendary Pete Seeger on his 90th birthday.

Havens once told an interviewer that, "I really sing songs that move me. I make a distinction between me and a lot of my friends. I am not in show business and never was. I'm in the communications business. That's what it is about for me." He died in April, 2013. He was 72.

The popular online black publication, *the Grio*, asked me to write a remembrance of Havens and assess his significance to music and history. This gave me the opportunity to say what I wanted to say four decades ago when I saw him and got hooked on his music. I wrote this. "Havens more than showed that with his music and his never-tiring dedication and passion to the cause of peace and civil rights. He was truly the universal man."

*****

In the fall of 1972, another musical sound created a big stir. It was directly tied in to a new genre of films dubbed *Blaxploitation* films. The formula action plots in these films always had a bigger than life black superhero outwitting and outfighting inept white villains. Black audiences loved them and packed the theaters to see them. The one film in this series that stood head and shoulders above the rest was the film *Superfly*. It was directed by famed photographer Gordon Parks, Jr. Ron O'Neal played the lead character *Youngblood Priest*, who had made a small fortune dealing cocaine, and enjoyed the glamorized fast life of women, fine clothes, and showy luxury cars. The twist is that Priest, panged by his conscious at exploiting blacks by hooking them on dope was trying to get out of the business. It was the music that not only made the film, but skyrocketed the composer and the performer of the music to a new height.

Two years after *Superfly* had made its smash debut, I finally corralled Curtis Mayfield backstage at the close of his concert at the Santa Monica Civic Auditorium. He was not just the man who wrote the music to *Superfly*, Mayfield had established a firm reputation as the griot of the black consciousness movement. He was an award winning songwriter, and had established his reputation as the lead singer with the popular R&B group *the Impressions* in the 1960s. He had become a strong musical voice in the civil rights movement. We had virtually adopted his *We're a Winner*, *Move on Up* and *Keep on Pushing* as the unofficial anthems that we played repeatedly at Black Student Union meetings in 1968 and 1969. I wanted to talk to him about the success of and the controversy over *Superfly*. The lyrics had been condemned by some as glorifying drugs, dope, sex, violence, and exploiting women.

Mayfield in his soft, sing song high voice just shook his head in bewilderment at the criticism. He insisted that they expressed the feelings, mood and conditions of many blacks in poor communities. He also said that the life Priest (O'Neal) led and the longing for that life as a ticket to get out of the ghetto for many impoverished blacks was a legitimate longing. His take on the songs shattered the romantic notion I had of the plight of many poor blacks. I had turned them into caricatures, and downtrodden victims. I could not fathom them as being victimizers on their own desolate turf. Mayfield saw that aspect of life in poor black communities. He captured that in the lyrics. He did not apologize for it to me. We talked for a few more minutes about other projects that he had in the pipeline and his upcoming tour on the East Coast after his Santa Monica appearance.

I got the eye from his PR man that Mayfield had to leave. He was quickly whisked away. In 1990, I was shocked at the news that Mayfield had been nearly killed when stage lighting equipment fell on him at an outdoor concert at Wingate Field in Flatbush, Brooklyn, New York. It left him paralyzed from the neck down. Though he continued to compose and win awards for his compositions, he performed little. He died three years later in December 1999. He was 57.

Mayfield had created a sensation with the *Superfly* soundtrack. Yet, his music was much more than that heard on one popular and controversial album. It was so rich, varied, and contained such moving messages about the black struggle it would stand the test of time and would make him an immortal, not just in the musical world, but as a social conscious artist.

*****

It was a cool July 10 night at the Hollywood Bowl in 1970. There was not an empty seat in the Bowl for the man who had long been hailed as a living legend. It was the first time I had seen or heard Miles Davis. However, the stories about his temperament, irascibility, and unpredictability were story book. Miles fiercely marched to his own tune. He showed that that evening at the Bowl. He paced the stage for a few minutes, playing a few notes here and there, seemingly oblivious to the audience. Then he would saunter back stage for what seemed like an eternity, still oblivious to the audience, while his back-up band filled in and wailed away. Then he'd repeat this again. There'd be a little toot from the trumpet back stage and Miles would drift back on stage. He never stayed out more than a few minutes at a time. Then midway through the concert, he didn't come out at all. Many in the crowd had grown restless by then and had a quizzical collective and exasperated look. There were a few scattered boos.

As the crowd filed out, some had the look that said they felt they'd been cheated. I was one of them. I was angered at Miles's blatant contempt for an admiring audience. However, that was Miles. My consolation was that I had not only seen the genius perform in person, and as thousands of others had through the years, I had experienced his don't give a damn temperament that night. I could forgive Miles. After all, he gave us *Bitches Brew and Jack Johnson.* The albums were released in September, 1970 and 1971. These albums took jazz in a whole direction. Their fusion of rock, electronic music, funk, and jazz would have a big influence on rock and funk music for the next decade and beyond. I loved it and practically wore the groves out on them.

Many of the old line jazz aficionados weren't so kind. They hammered Miles as abandoning the classic jazz that had made him the leading jazz name and performer of the 1950s and 1960s. Miles was undaunted by the criticism and made his bow in 1971 to the black consciousness wave that had gripped many blacks. His touring ensemble now included young black sidemen and they invariably appeared clad in Dashikis. Two of them, Leon "Ndugu" Chancellor and James Mtume I frequently heard play with their own groups after they left Miles in 1975.

Some years later, Mtume had transitioned to a part time host of a popular black oriented talk show on KISS Radio in New York. Whenever I was in New York, I'd sit in on the show with Mtume and the other hosts to discuss topical racial issues. We occasionally talked about his work with Miles. Mtume cherished that time with him and his influence on him and other young back musicians then and thereafter. Miles died in September, 1991. He was 65. His place as jazz innovator, critic, and all-time legend was secure. That was Miles's genius. I even forgave him again for that night at the Bowl.

*****

A few years later it was just the opposite at a Ray Charles concert at a club in the San Fernando Valley. Whereas Miles was barely on stage at the Bowl, Ray Charles, it seemed, would never leave the stage. He ripped through some of his most popular old standards and roused the audience with the perennial favorite *Georgia.* In between, he chattered to the audience in that familiar raspy voice. Charles was having a ball on stage. He couldn't get enough of the audience as he took us on his musical stroll down memory lane. I edged as close to the stage as I could to get a close look at him. I was fascinated watching him bob and weave his head back in a perfect arc. This was a move that Charles had patented. It was just a joy to watch up close.

There were reports that Charles had been in ill health, and this had forced him for a time from the performance stage. None of this was in evidence that night. His concert stretched out in time. He seemed determined to squeeze every moment he could out of his time on stage. Charles lived up to his bill as the master showman. He gave an audience their money's worth.

During the next decade, Ray's music was heard less and less as musical tastes changed. That changed in the 1980s with his appearance in the film, *The Blues Brothers*. Ray was suddenly "rediscovered" again. The Charles revival got even bigger when he appeared in a series of Diet Pepsi commercials. Now he was a hit with younger audiences. He died in June, 2004. He was 73. In 2004, Jaime Foxx portrayed Charles in the biopic, *Ray*. He won the Academy Award for the role. It was much deserved. Foxx's performance was so compelling that I even thought he was Charles.

When I left the club after Ray Charles's concert thirty years earlier, I left it with a smile and a deep appreciation for the man who like Miles wore the mantle and title well of "genius."

I only caught Charles and Miles once in performance. However, I caught the Godfather of Soul in person twice. The first time was at the L.A. Shrine Auditorium in July, 1968. He was a bundle of raw primal energy on stage. He brought the crowd to its feet with his band's pulsating beat, his trademark lyrics and songs, and his unparalleled stage showmanship. It was different the next time.

More than thirty years had passed. I watched with regret an aging, slowed down, Brown pace laboriously at the Greek Theater in July, 2002. He was restrained and measured in his dance moves, and sparing in the number of songs he performed. However, he had lost none of his old flair and his old standards were sure fire audience pleasers. The concert was as always in the past, part party and a part oldies remembrance.

Much had happened to Brown in between the first time that I saw him perform live and the last time. The cocaine binges, the domestic assaults on his wife, the wild chase fleeing from the police in South Carolina after allegedly shooting at a police officer, and the subsequent three year prison sentence he received were well-known. This didn't totally diminish Brown's luster or his stature. He had reigned supreme too long as the Godfather of soul and he had too many R&B classics that millions still remembered for that to happen.

In August, 2014, I attended the first day opening of the biopic, *Get on Up,* on Brown starring Chadwick Boseman as Brown. I was impressed. Boseman captured almost to perfection Brown's signature dance moves and the soulful rendition of his best known hits. It was almost as if it was the James Brown that I saw often reincarnated on the big screen. The Godfather would have been pleased.

He died on Christmas, 2006. He was 73.

There were two concerts that I attended that were unforgettable. The first was the summer night in 1982 at the Hollywood Bowl that the Temptations came together in L.A. in what had been billed as their "reunion" concert. The bowl was one stop on their celebrated reunion tour. It brought together the then current and several of the original members of the Motown group. I, like many, had grown up listening and dancing to the Temptations hits during the 1960s. We had heard and sung the lyrics so often that they were indelibly burned in our memory.

The Temptations were like family and that night we greeted them like loving family members. The instant the music signaled one of the tunes, the Temps barely opened their mouths to sing, when the audience as if on cue, sang in unison with them. It was one gigantic mass sing along. The 1960s may have passed. But the Temptations enduring musical legacy never would.

*****

The other concert that had special meaning for me was in August 1983 at the Greek Theater in Los Angeles. It was a concert that I almost missed and would have if it hadn't been for the insistence of a friend who at the last minute talked me into going. It was an almost exact repeat of the Temptations concert. When Marvin Gaye came out on stage in his resplendent white suit, and hit the first note of *Distant Lover*, the audience went crazy. They sang the words along with him. Gaye had a reputation for being notoriously shy. Word was that it was a struggle to get him on stage. But once on stage it was an even bigger struggle to get him off. He roared through his old hits and nearly all from his then new album *Sexual Healing* and *Midnight Lover*. His sensuous, silky, high pitched voice sent the audience into a swoon. Midway through, he tore off his jacket and tie, and he glided from one end of the stage to the other, pouring feeling and soul into every note. I felt transported to another dimension by the sound, the vibes and the energy. This was the second time that I had that surreal experience listening to Gaye.

The other was at the NBA all-star game at the Inglewood Forum in February 1983. Three decades after that game people still talk about it, not the game, that's largely forgotten. They talk about what Gaye did when he took the mic and sang the Star Spangled Banner. The arrangement of it was like none other heard up until then. The R&B rhythmic drum beat, the lilting and rising tones from Gaye, and his impassioned rolling of the words to the anthem stunned the players and the crowd. I watched the players leap, shout and high five each other when the full effect of what they had heard and witnessed sunk in. The audience was inflamed by it and clapped and stomped in appreciation for several minutes. Gaye strode off the court resplendent in his white suit as he acknowledged the applause. It was a rendition of the Star Spangled Banner that I had first heard a month earlier.

I thought about that night at the Greek Theatre and the Forum six months later on April 1, 1984 when Gaye who was one day shy of his 45th birthday was shot dead by his father in a domestic altercation. Marvin was a superlative, even revolutionary, voice and talent. I ranked his *Whats Going On* with its explicit socially conscious message and creative use of instrumentation and voice, alongside the Beatle's *Sargent Peppers Lonely Heart Clubs Band* as the two greatest pop musical albums of all time.

It gave me great pleasure to organize a twentieth anniversary tribute to Gaye at his star on Hollywood Blvd in 2004. As was the case that magical night at the Greek Theater in 1983, fans and Gaye family members came from far and wide in memory and celebration of the man and his music that would never die.

Marvin Gaye, James Brown, Ray Charles, the Temptations, and Miles Davis were immortals in the world of music during their lives. They had a marvelous capacity to grow, and change with and adapt to the times. They invented and reinvented themselves as needed and could not be forgotten. There were others who accomplished the same feat in music and the arts. I witnessed their feats too.

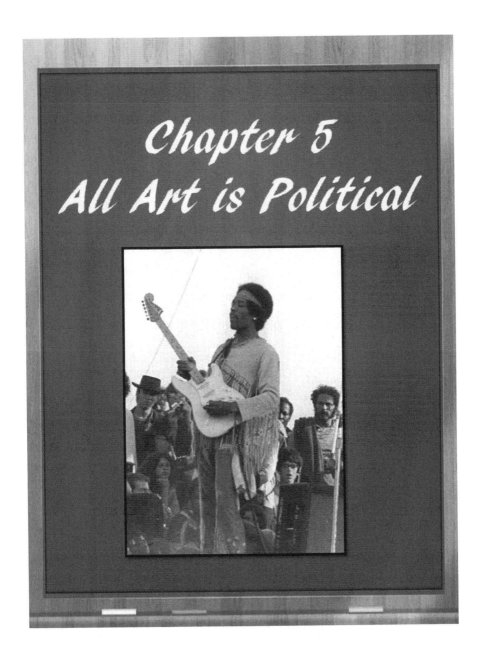

Chapter 5 - All Art Is Political

I was near catatonic after leaving a press screening of the film *Woodstock* at a theater in Hollywood in March 1970. The film captured the three Days of what was billed as a festival of "Peace & Music" held at Max Yasgur's 600-acre dairy farm in the Catskills near the hamlet of White Lake in the town of Bethel, New York, from August 15 to 18, 1969. It featured a virtual Who's Who of pop and rock music notables of that age.

There was one musician who did one number in the film that snapped me to instant attention. It came toward the end of the film. It was a rendition of the Star Spangled Banner that I had ever heard before. The electronic guitar notes to it rose and fell, soared and dipped, and he played it with a studied, almost dead pan expression. I knew I had witnessed a musician like few other. I also knew that when I attended Jimi Hendrix's concert at the Inglewood Forum in July, 1969. I would not be attending a concert but an event.

I had seats in the front row. Long before he took the stage the place was jammed. There were 17,000 others there and they were just as eager to hear Hendrix. In his hour long concert he massaged, stroked, petted, and rubbed his guitar between his legs, dropped to the floor and picked at the strings with his teeth. Every note was in place. It was not a musical but an erotic experience. He played and sang the gamut of musical style, blues, hard rock, R&B, ballads. He then dropped in his signature piece, the pulsating, other worldly irreverent rendition of the Star Spangled Banner.

Hendrix spoke very little. He preferred to let his guitar and vocals speak for themselves, and did they. He was everything that I expected. He had revolutionized guitar playing. He combined sheer brilliant musical artistry, with consummate showmanship. Like many of the musical greats, he knew how to grab an audience. He placed an indelible imprint on my musical listening that night. I couldn't get enough of Hendrix after that. I would play *Purple Haze* and *Red House* until the grooves on the album practically wore thin.

My Hendrix mania could not be sated. I caught him twice more. The next time was again at the Forum. He had briefly jettisoned his British sidemen, Noel Redding and Mitch Mitchell, and had gone into his brief black power phase. His sidemen for this concert were drummer Buddy Miles and bassist Billy Cox, both African-American. The last time I saw him was at an outdoor concert at Devonshire Downs in the San Fernando Valley. He gave the same riveting, stirring performance that exuded sex on stage. There was the same, massive gale of penetrating sound from the stage.

In September 1970, I started my graduate studies at Cornell's Africana Studies Program. I hadn't been there more than one week when I got the news that Hendrix had died of an overdose in London. He was 37. The news of his death hit me hard as I knew it did thousands of others. I was sad and angered in part because he was so young, and in greater part because of the personal stamp his music had made on me. I had seen him, not once, but three times. Each time, I realized that Hendrix was more than a musical genius. He was as Gaye, a transformative force in music and society. There's talk of making the definitive film on Hendrix. I'm sure that will eventually happen. I will watch it whenever it's made. It will bring back the joyful memory of that night at the Forum in 1969, when Hendrix transported me to a dimension in sound that few others have done since.

*****

The late 1960s and the better part of the 1970s was a time when artists provided not only great entertainment but great inspiration as well. Their performances were not just performances in the strict sense of the term, but events; events that were always memorable. As a reporter and feature writer for the *Free Press* and later Pacifica Radio during those years, I mixed my attendance at many concerts and film openings with interviews with the stars and performers. I attended multiple concerts of comedians Richard Pryor, and Moms Mabley, did a backstage interview with Eartha Kitt, and a restaurant interview with actor Paul Winfield after the release of the film *Sounder* that he starred in along with Cicely Tyson.

The second and most memorable Pryor concert I attended was at the Wiltern Theater in L.A. in 1979. The concert was a turning point for Pryor, the audience and me. Midway through this rapid fire, irreverent profanity laced cracks, quips and monologue; he stopped, reflected a moment, and then announced that he had purged the word *Nigger* from his routine. A stunned and perplexed audience listened in silence as he explained that he had had an epiphany. The epiphany had come during a trip to Africa that year. Pryor later related the story of what happened in his autobiography. He said that as he sat in a hotel lobby and saw "gorgeous black people, like everyplace else we'd been. The only people you saw were black at the hotel, on television, in stores, on the street, in the newspapers, at restaurants, running the government, on advertisements. Everywhere." Pryor then said to his wife: "You know what? There are no niggers here... The people here, they still have their self-respect, their pride." He saw the beauty, wonder, and dignity of the people he met during his trip he was moved to tears by the horrid history of enslavement. Therefore, he could no longer justify using the penultimate derogatory word about blacks.

As Pryor's words slowly sank in at the concert, several in the audience clapped, and then it became a torrent of applause. Pryor had touched a nerve with his revelatory announcement. It was his acknowledgement of pride in his history, heritage and self. The use of a word so demeaning, psychically destructive, and dehumanizing no longer had any place in a comedy routine, at least not his.

Pryor's on stage epiphany took me back more than a decade to another performance I attended at a downtown L.A. theater. Jackie Moms Mabley was the featured act that evening. The list of black comic greats of the day was long Red Foxx, Godfrey Cambridge, Pigmeat Markham, George Kirby, Flip Wilson and a bevy of others. Moms, though, ranked right at the top. She never stooped to use profanity to shock or make demeaning characterizations or put downs of African-Americans to get laughs. Moms shuffled on stage with her characteristic lazy, slow gait, dressed in a rumpled house dress and floppy hat. Before she uttered a word, there was a torrent of laughter from the crowd. She just stood there for what seemed forever grinning and laughing. When the laughter died down she chortled out as if her false teeth were stuck in her gums, her stock line "the only thing an old man can bring me is the phone number of a young man."

Her humorous look and stage presence was so infectious that even if she didn't have any funny lines you'd still laugh. In the concert, she riffed continually on old and young men and the audience was in stitches. Moms would slide in a line or two about racial discrimination and how it had to be combatted. She and the other greats of her day were practitioners of clean comedy before anyone thought to put that term to it. Moms had lived up to her moniker as "The Funniest Woman in the World". The evening I saw her and after her passing in 1975, she was 81, I felt that yet another of the greats of the golden age of black comedy had left us. They left a legacy that would endure.

*****

The smile I saw on Eartha Kitt's face backstage at the Aquarius Theater in Hollywood that late spring afternoon in 1978 was memorable. It belied the pain, ridicule and turmoil she had endured after she was unceremoniously shoved at or near the top of then President Lyndon Johnson's enemies list in January, 1968. That seemed to be the furthest thing from her mind when she greeted me at the Theater. Kitt was in Los Angeles starring in her tour production of the musical *Timbuktu*. I was assigned to do a brief interview and a review of the production.

Kitt's smile and energy melted the awe and nervousness that I felt at being up close too and actually talking with an entertainment legend. Then there was the "incident." That was the furor that Kitt had ignited when she denounced the Vietnam War and poverty to Johnson at a White House luncheon in January, 1968. A decade later the controversy still got the tongues wagging.

Her performance in Los Angeles was in part Kitt's American scene entertainment rehabilitation after being virtually banned in the U.S. after her Johnson White House outburst. Her performance was also in part a brash effort to reclaim the luster that had made her virtually a household name and an icon in the entertainment world in the 1950s and early 1960s. By then Kitt had firmly established her legacy as an award winning internationally acclaimed singer, dancer, film, stage and TV actress. She was tagged as sultry, sensual, and sexual alluring. That was the surface stuff. Kitt's brash, sassy, and high energy style and persona sent the clear message that she was her own woman. She refused to be relegated to the stereotypical stage and film roles, and turned her sensuality into a badge of fierce independence and pride, the trademark of defiance. Her pioneer independence and sense of self influenced the coming generation of young female entertainers and personalities from Oprah to Beyonce to Madonna. They owe her a debt of gratitude.

This side of Kitt obscured the Kitt who was passionately devoted to and supported peace and civil rights causes. The clash with Johnson, really the Johnsons, Lyndon and Lady Bird Johnson, at the celebrity women's luncheon in January 1968 gave the first public hint of that.

Lady Bird Johnson had invited Kitt to the luncheon and in an innocent moment asked her what she thought about the problems of inner city youth. She didn't mince words and lambasted the Johnson administration for not doing more about poverty, joblessness, and drugs in black communities. Kitt didn't stop there, she tied her outburst directly into an attack on the Vietnam War, and a war she said was without reason or explanation. Her verbal assault on the war and racial problems made headline news. A badly shaken first lady and an enraged LBJ denounced her. The next few years she was hounded and harassed by the FBI, the IRS and Secret Service agents. The CIA even compiled a gossipy, intrusive dossier on her that attempted to paint her as a sex starved malcontent. The public storm and the negative press proved too much.

Her career was effectively dead in the United States. She stuck by her guns, though, and did not apologize, retract or soften her criticism of Johnson's war and racial policies. Kitt in fact hadn't said anything at that luncheon that thousands of others hadn't said about Johnson's hopelessly failed, flawed and losing war and racial problems. The difference was who said it; namely a celebrated star, and where it was said at the White House. She took the heat and paid the price for giving an honest opinion and her deep felt belief about the cause of peace and social justice. She was branded as a racial agitator.

Missed in the overreaching hysteria and the vindictive bashing was that underneath the glitter and carefully crafted sexpot image, Kitt had given time and money to the NAACP and other civil rights organizations. She supported and participated in the March on Washington. During her wilderness years when she was forced to work outside the U.S. she took heat for performing before all white audiences in South Africa. But like so much about Kitt that went unnoticed, she broke barriers by insisting that her cast was integrated. She also quietly raised money for black schools in the country.

During our brief talk in the afternoon backstage at the Aquarius, Kitt spent as much time talking about her devotion to the civil rights movement and the injustice of apartheid in South Africa, than about the production she was in. She did not mince words when I gingerly asked her about the "incident." She laughed but did not express any regret about what she said and did that day at the White House. She expressed no bitterness about the years of media and public ostracism. When we finished I thanked her, and thought again that I had just spoken to a woman, a grand woman, who had suffered mightily for her beliefs and outspokenness but was still singing, and performing. She had weathered the storm.

I took pride in placing flowers on the top of her star on Hollywood Blvd the day after she passed on Christmas in 2008. She was 80. This was the Eartha Kitt, the impassioned contributor to peace and civil rights that I knew, and paid homage to that day.

"C'est si bon"

*****

Their careers did not have the politically painful twists, turns and tragedy of Kitt but they had their share of drama. Both women came to be known and admired for much more than their song. By the time I saw Nina Simone at the Black Panther unity rally at the L.A. Sports Arena in February 1968, she had earned the title the high priestess of soul. Her signature hit *Mississippi Goddamn* had shocked many listeners with its unabashed, raw protest message. She wrote it as a response to the murder of Medgar Evers in June 1963 and the bombing of a church in Birmingham, Alabama in 1963 that killed four black children. It was boycotted in certain southern states at the time and the lyrics told why.

Simone had accomplished a remarkable feat with it. Not only was it a strident message of protest against racism. It was also a commercial success. When she sang it in concert as she always did the audience went ballistic. Three weeks after her appearance at the Sports Arena rally, I saw her at Doug Weston's Troubadour club in Hollywood. She wasted no time and led off with the song. She drew every word out for all its biting worth. She was tough, earthy, and phenomenally electric. There was a freshness and vibrancy in her art that had a strong appeal to me.

I wasn't alone. More than 100 artists; rappers, folk, country and western, R&B, jazz, and musical composers have said that Simone influenced them. The sheer number of top artists influenced by her music and style is a lasting testament to her musical impact. Simone more than earned the title "High Priestess of Soul" not by her musical artistry alone but by her uncompromising dedication to the movement for social justice. She gave unsparingly of her time and talent to that cause. She passed in April 2003. She was 70. The speakers at her funeral included many of those such as Ossie Davis and Sonia Sanchez who like Simone had given unsparingly to the cause of social justice and the black arts and literary movement. They all said as much in their tributes to her. I deeply appreciated their words. I said them myself after seeing her.

One of those who attended Simone's funeral service also had a profound impact on musical styles. She made as strong a commitment to civil rights and the movement for social justice as Simone. Though Miriam Makeba travelled a different path than Nina in her early years, her dedication and commitment to social causes was never in question. I saw her at one of her early concerts in this country in the early 1970s. The clicking sound that she made in her songs was traditional in her native Xhosa language.

It was a captivating sound with her clipped South African accent. She later titled one of her songs "The Click Song" ("Qongqothwane" in Xhosa). She was a regal presence on stage. Her marriage to Stokely Carmichael in 1968, seemed the perfect welding of two cultures, African and black American, as well as the radical black movement. I would catch a news item every now and then about Makeba that she had been recognized by the UN for her charitable work in the fight against hunger, had returned from her exile to South Africa in 1990, and had released an album of new songs.

I would catch her again in a brief appearance near the end of her performance career when she appeared at West Angeles Church in Los Angeles in 2005 Though she was far removed from the concert stage by then, the fire and magnetism that had made her such a name and presence in the 1960s and 1970s was still very much present. Her passion in song had brought her an enthusiastic embrace by blacks in America. She was the musical bridge between the mirror image struggle of blacks in South Africa and America against racial oppression.

The woman that came to be called "Mama Africa" died in November 2008. She was 76. To the end, she continued to remember and recount the pain, suffering and sacrifice made by so many against apartheid and for social justice. She and other South African freedom fighters can be heard telling that story in the 2002 documentary *Amandla!: A Revolution in Four-Part Harmony*. I watched it and applauded it and her once again.

*****

I also attended many press movie preview film openings in the 1970s. By then Hollywood had begun to discover that films could be made with blacks in dramatic roles. These movies could have blacks in the major roles, other than the shoot em' up, violence lace, or slapstick comic and *Blaxploitation* films and draw crossover audiences. The film *Sounder* was one of them. It was released in 1972 and it told the story of an African-American boy living with his sharecropper family and their trials and tribulations as they struggled against poverty and racism in the Jim Crow South.

The mother was played by Cicely Tyson. She had already racked up many screen and stage accolades. The father, played by Paul Winfield, was less known but he was an up and comer. A few days after the press screening, I met him at the ancient actor's restaurant hang out, the Musso & Frank Grill in Hollywood in October 1972. Winfield was alone and sat very unobtrusively at a corner table when I arrived. I apologized for being late. He said not to pay it any mind. I asked him what it meant to him personally to star in a black family-themed movie and whether he thought it would lead to other major and serious screen opportunities for him and other black actors. Winfield understood that one film for a black actor especially a serious drama part might not be the instant path to open up an industry that through much of its history had demeaned, ignored, and mocked blacks in film.

Yet, he was optimistic that things were changing, and that Hollywood was slowly getting the message that blacks and others hungered to see themselves in serious roles, and that these movies could be box office successes. Winfield's final word to me was that it was inevitable that new, younger blacks would in time make their mark in Hollywood. I thought to myself as he said that that one of them would undoubtedly be named Winfield. He and Tyson made history by being the first black male and female to be nominated for an Academy Award in the same film, *Sounder*.

I was right about Winfield. His career flourished for years in the industry. He would land a number of meaty roles. Winfield was the first of what would be a steady procession of black actors to make the breakthrough in films he predicted to me would come. I thought of that prediction the day it was announced that he had died of a heart attack in March, 2004. He was 64.

I thought about how he helped pave the way for the breakthrough of blacks to get more substantial parts in Hollywood films by his own amazing work in the industry. Blacks in the business owed him thanks for that.

*****

On August 14, 2002 I received an urgent call from Claire Luna, a staff writer for the *Los Angeles Times*. She said that she was writing the paper's obituary on Alfred Ligon. He had passed after a long illness. He was 96. Given his health challenges which I was well aware of, his passing was not a total surprise. Luna wanted my impressions of Mr. Ligon and his significance to the black literary and arts scene in Los Angeles and the nation. This gave me great pleasure. Here's how she quoted me: "For Los Angeles writer Earl Ofari Hutchinson, who started visiting the shop as a Los Angeles City College student in 1963, the store and its resources were a revelation at a time when Southern California was isolated from the civil rights mainstream.

"He created an environment of comfort and intellectual stimulation," Hutchinson said. "There were no pretensions about him, no ivory tower intellectualism. He strongly felt he had a duty to really be a solid mentor to young people and point them in the right direction in terms of understanding their past."

My comment was no exaggeration. The Aquarian Spiritual Center that Ligon, and his wife Bernice, founded in 1941 was the country's oldest continuously operated black-owned bookstore. But it was much more than that. It was also a meeting place on the West Coast for two decades for a new crop of black militant activists during the ferment of the civil rights and black consciousness movement in the 1960s. There were innumerable meetings, discussion groups and conferences there with fierce discussion and debates on the issues of the day. It was also a place where many of the new and upcoming black writers could discuss their books. The list of authors that read and signed books at the Aquarian read like a world class who's who of major writers such as Maya Angelou, Amiri Baraka, Terry McMillan, and Walter Mosely.

One author perhaps more than any of the others had turned a book signing there into a landmark cultural and media event. I knew that it would be a mob scene at the center the day Alex Haley was scheduled to sign his newly released *Roots* at the center. By then *Roots*, published in 1976, was well ensconced at the top of every top ten book list. Haley had signed a blockbuster deal with ABC-TV to turn the book in to what would become the most watched series in TV history at that point with millions glued to the set. The day before Haley's scheduled appearance I talked with Bernice to make sure that I could get a seat in the receiving area at the entrance of the store. She assured me that it would not be a problem.

I got there an hour before his arrival time. The line of those waiting stretched a block long. The police had erected barriers at a couple of points on the street near the center. I flashed my KPFK press pass and squeezed through the line. Bernice waved me in. Haley was running late, but there were no grumbles from the crowd. Most people waiting believed that they were part of history that day. Most clutched one even two copies of *Roots* tightly as if it was a long lost treasure or precious family heir loom. Haley's autograph on their book(s) was worth more than gold to them, it was a historical rendering of the plight of black families in America before during and after slavery.

I knew Haley had arrived even before he walked in from the loud applause and cheers that went up from the crowd. By then it stretched for two blocks. Haley had a broad grin when he walked in and greeted Bernice and Ligon warmly. There was no affection or pretense of assumed importance. He seemed genuinely pleased to be there. Bernice had said before that he had a tight schedule, and had a luncheon and two other engagements that afternoon, and he had limited time.

You couldn't tell it. He interspersed his signings with constant banter with his admirers. Two attendants whose job it was to insure that the line kept moving anxiously glanced at their watches. Haley seemed oblivious to them and time when they would occasionally step in to gently remind an individual who wanted to stop and dally a little too long and invariably tell Haley an anecdote about their family. Haley ignored their admonition to them to rush along. He thanked them almost apologetically for having to rush them past after he signed their book.

What Haley's PR agent thought would be a tight hour crept past that time. The steady procession of autograph seekers showed no sign of ending. Haley seemed to be energized by the effusive praise, near adulation and grateful thanks he got from the crowd. Finally, one of the PR persons, abruptly and with a note of finality said that they had to leave. Haley was still signing as he rose from the chair. He turned slowly and thanked the Ligons for the signing and shook their hand.

I had hoped to have a moment to discuss his writings, the book, and his reaction to the public success of it. I knew from the looks of the PR agents that wouldn't happen. I contented myself with a handshake. As dozens of others did I thanked him for *Roots* and wished him the best. Haley smiled and said he appreciated that. He slowly walked out the door to the pats on the shoulder, and cheers from those who had lingered to get one final glimpse of him.

Haley had not only written a history of slavery and struggle for the ages but had tapped a longing in millions of African-Americans who thirsted for some connect with their family past. Slavery had been the great void that the unknown family past of generations of African-Americans had fallen into. *Roots* was Haley's bid to partially fill that void. It would eventually be published in 37 languages, garner a special Pulitzer Prize for him and the record breaking series on ABC that was watched by an estimated 130 million viewers. I thanked the Ligons for doing their part not just in bringing Haley to our community but for all their work over the years to fill the void in our historical past. I know Haley certainly appreciated that as well and he told them so.

There would be controversy over how much of *Roots* was based on actual fact. And how much was invention by Haley. That didn't change one fact. Haley had written a book for the ages; a book that inspired thousands of African-Americans to try to fill in the missing pages of family histories obliterated by slavery. Haley was comfortable with what he had done and the book's success. He reportedly was once asked if he had known how successful *Roots* would become would he have done anything differently. He didn't hesitate, "yes, I would have written faster." Controversy or no, Haley was comfortable with what he had accomplished and never looked back. Haley died in February, 1992. He was 70.

*****

There was another part to the story of the Aquarium Bookstore and Center. This part was tragic and triumphant. Dozens of buildings in Los Angeles went up in flames following the acquittal of the four LAPD officers that beat Rodney King in April 1992. One of those was located in a mini shopping center. It housed the Aquarium. When I got a call that the Aquarium was in ashes, I rushed to the site. I held an impromptu press conference at the site. I implored the community to contribute to a rebuilding fund to restore the bookstore. Within minutes after several TV stations broadcast the appeal, my phone line lit up.

Callers asked what they could do and where they could contribute money. I gave people the Ligon's number and urged them to contact them for details. Within days after the fund drive kicked into high gear, a consortium of independent bookstores joined in. Ultimately, more than $70,000 was raised for the store's rebuilding.

Author Maya Angelou was one of the first in the door to offer her name and support to the effort. This was more than a generous offer to help from a woman who had attained phenomenal success in the literary world and had racked up nearly every major award and prize for her poignant and inspiring poetry, novels, essays, TV and drama works, and her many autobiographies. Her first autobiography *I Know Why the Caged Bird Sings* published in 1969 easily ranked in the first tier of all time American classics.

The attacks it elicited were a perverse, back door tribute to the book's importance. Hardly a year passed in which a self-appointed guardian of public morals group somewhere would demand that the book be pulled from a library and banned from a classroom for its depictions of lesbianism, premarital cohabitation, pornography, and violence. I chuckled when I read about these petty diatribes against her and her book. As a writer, I always delighted when I was attacked. That's when I knew I was doing my job. That is to stir someone's brain cells to the point where they're either mad at me or themselves for something I said.

Angelou was much more than a literary leading light. She was an activist. This is what made me take note of her during the 1970s. Her years living in Africa, her friendship and working relationship with Malcolm X, her work with Dr. King, and her solid credentials as an uncompromising outspoken advocate of black expression in the arts made her a force to be reckoned with far beyond the literary world. I cheered any writer that put their time, talent, and their pen on the line for social justice. This was my kind of writer. Angelou was exactly that kind of writer.

Unfortunately, I missed her the infrequent times that she spoke and presented her readings in Los Angeles in the decade after the Aquarium burned down. I was determined to correct that. In April 2002, I received a notice that she would be speaking and giving a reading at the Arlington Theater in Santa Barbara. I had my chance. Barbara and I decided to make a weekend of it. So we drove to Santa Barbara the afternoon before her presentation at the theater that night. There was not an empty seat in the house. Seemingly every top city official turned out for her appearance. After a brief introduction, Angelou took a seat on the stage and held forth with anecdotes, stories, recited poetry, and read from her works.

The applause was exuberant. She had taken the city by storm that night. She provided the audience with a trove of insights into the heart and soul of one of America's literary and social activist treasures. She was the African-American artist supremely dedicated to their craft as well as the struggle against racial injustice. In the years after, Angelou was a ubiquitous presence on the national scene; writing, speaking, and lecturing. She worked tirelessly for Bill Clinton in 1992 and Obama's election in 2008. She continued to do what she was born to do write, write, and write. Even though her health had declined, she was still working on yet another autobiography about her experiences with national and world leaders. She had much to tell there.

The day of her death in May 2014, she was 86, a number of reporters called to get my thoughts on her death. I spoke as one writer and activist assessing another writer and activist. This made it easy to tell what Angelou meant to me and the ages. I said and later wrote "She was simply the best and brightest of us." I knew exactly why. Angelou always sang my song.

Chapter 6
A Tale of Two
Politicians

Chapter 6 - A Tale of Two Politicians

If there were ever two American politicians that it could be said were the polar opposites of each other in the 1960s in their background, political philosophy, and especially on racial issues, it was George C. Wallace and Adam Clayton Powell, Jr. In the span of six months in 1968 I would stand and sit at arms-length from both men. It started out as a youthful prank, a lark. One of the members of the Black Student Union at Cal State L.A. had picked up a flyer that announced that George Wallace would be speaking at Cal Tech's Beckman Auditorium in Pasadena in October, 1968. He said almost half jokingly as we walked to the Student Union, the day before his scheduled appearance, why don't we go.

I was incredulous at the suggestion. But he was persistent and he wasn't kidding. I thought about it and the idea of being in the same auditorium with Wallace and his rabid followers grew on me. I said why not. By then Wallace had become major news and a real political threat to the Democrats in the 1968 presidential campaign. He had broken from the Democrats and formed his pro-state's rights, veiled race baiting, American Independent Party. He was poised to throw a monkey wrench in the Democrat's fragile presidential election campaign machinery.

The Wallace, though, of 1968 was from appearances not the defiant, fire eating, rabid segregationist, and overt race baiting Wallace of 1963. That was the Wallace who in his inaugural address on taking the oath of office as Alabama governor shouted "I say segregation now, segregation tomorrow, and segregation forever." With those words Wallace gained instant infamy and for the next three years as the civil rights fight moved headlong into Alabama, he did everything he could to back up his words.

The Wallace of 1968 had become a major national political player and had morphed into a savvy, shrewd, and expert tactical politician. He had institutionalized racial code speak. He had expunged any direct reference to race from his stump vocabulary. The enemy now was big government, pointy headed Washington bureaucrats, and unwarranted federal intrusion in people's lives. Wallace cynically rode and in turn stoked the massive tide of the white backlash to civil rights protests, the urban riots, the perceived breakdown in law and order, and militant anti-Vietnam war protests. He parlayed that into thousands of white votes in the North, and a viable presidential bid through his American Independent Party. The party had hundreds of grassroots followers, organizers, and funders throughout the nation. He also had drawn a sizeable following among young voters. The October 3, 1968 edition of the Cal Tech student newspaper I picked up at Cal Tech appealed for the "youth of America to back the courageous, constructive leadership of George C. Wallace." It offered a free subscription, the "Youth for Wallace" newsletter.

*****

I noted the light air of euphoria in the crowd as I walked toward the front entrance of the auditorium. A small army of police and campus security guards had ringed the entrance and the building. There was a row of tables stacked with Wallace campaign materials, buttons and posters in the front. The crowd was not just the stereotypical caricatured snuff dipping, pot belly Confederate flag waving, rednecks, that were routinely depicted when describing Wallace supporters. In fact, there was not a Confederate flag in sight. American flags festooned the Wallace tables and the auditorium. The crowd was a mix of young persons, women, middle aged couples, college students and white collar business, and professional types. Some had brought their small children.

Our small group of four black students stuck out like a tiny island in the sea. There were no other blacks. When we got to the entrance, Wallace supporters flanked each side of the door. And one with a wry smile, took a hard look at us and said "Now you boys behave yourself." Did he think we were there to protest or disrupt? He did. It was a not so subtle warning. He didn't have to worry. Four against several thousand wasn't much of a match. To my surprise, we were able to move quickly through the crowd and we found seats near the front of the stage. The word had evidently gone out for Wallace staff and supporters to be on their best behavior. Those that stood nearby ignored us. There were no hostile glances, or derogatory remarks.

After a brief warmup introduction, Wallace sprinted out on the stage. He exuded energy and exuberance. The crowd went wild. They stomped, hooted, and cheered madly. Wallace smiled broadly, waved and quickly took the podium. He thanked the hosts and the audience for coming out. He said that their presence showed Washington that there was a new spirit in America and people were sending a message they were fed up with lawlessness, and an intrusive federal government.

Wallace was short, almost diminutive, and he seemed to lift up on his toes when he made a point that he wanted to drive home. The man in front of me was a demagogue who had fine-tuned his speaking craft and knew how to rev up an audience. There were a couple of times I was sure that he glanced directly at the four of us in the front. He seemed to have a smirk when he railed against the federal government infringing on the sovereign rights of people in the states. When he delivered his stock lines about restoring law and order the applause swelled. He brought the house down when he shouted that he just wished that a demonstrator would sit down on the street in front of his car, if he did he'd run him over. This brought more wild hoots and cheers. Wallace was in his element and played it up for all it was worth. He brought more shouts with his oft repeated line that, "There's not a dime's worth of difference between the Democratic and Republican parties."

He closed by exhorting the crowd to vote and send a strong message to the bureaucrats that the people were sick and tired of big government running their lives and sicker of the anarchy and violence in the streets. It was a *tour de force* performance. Not once did he utter the word race, let alone make any reference to blacks and civil rights. The applause was deafening when he finished. He bounded off the stage almost as if he were on jets, waving as he sped to the exit. The mood was electric in the crowd and we could barely hear each other above the din. Wallace had touched an emotional nerve. In a grudging way, I was impressed with his gripping, carefully crafted, and even toned pitches. They were simple, easily understandable and pandered to an audience that bought into the notion that civil rights, the riots, and were one and the same enemy.

Wallace didn't and couldn't win the presidency. But he won in two other ways. He got almost 10 million popular votes, carried five Southern states, and garnered 45 electoral votes plus one vote from an elector in 1968. He came fairly close to receiving enough votes to throw the presidential election to the House of Representatives. He won in another way too. Richard Nixon, Ronald Reagan, George H.W. Bush, and in a toned down way, Bill Clinton, lifted whole cloth Wallace's pet themes of reining in an alleged big, bloated stifling federal government, touting law and order, railing against liberal permissiveness, street crime, and backing tough draconian laws, and massive military defense.

On the drive back from the Wallace rally, we talked excitedly about how we had gone into the enemy's camp and come out in one piece. Wallace would survive an attempt on his life when he was shot five times by Arthur Bremer while campaigning at the Laurel Shopping Center in Laurel, Maryland on May 15, 1972. It left him paralyzed. He would later undergo an epiphany on race and renounce his segregationist past and even apologize to civil rights leaders. He died in September, 1998. He was 79.

The bitter truth remained that Wallace had capitalized on race baiting; turning it into a fine, and disguised art. This caused a cataclysmic change in American politics. I felt that shift as I stood a few feet from him as he spoke on that early fall evening in 1968.

*****

By the spring 1968, the administration at Cal State L.A. was under much pressure from the Black Student Union and other campus student organizations to invite controversial speakers to lecture regularly on campus. We lobbied hard to get one speaker whose whole life was marked by controversy. For more than three decades since his election in 1944 to Congress from Harlem, Adam Clayton Powell Jr. had been one of the most iconoclastic figures in American politics. He had cobbled his tenure as the fiery and outspoken minister of Harlem's famed Abyssinian Baptist Church into an unmatched power base among blacks.

In the 1930s, he organized and led mass meetings, **rent strikes**, and public campaigns against job and housing discrimination. Powell had so exacerbated President Harry Truman that reportedly in a moment of peek; Truman cursed Powell as "that damn nigger preacher." His long running chairmanship of the House Education and Labor Committee, and his relentless prodding of Lyndon Johnson to push hard to enact legislation combating poverty and for tougher civil rights laws enforcement made him a major political power broker. His flamboyant, skirt the edge of legality life style, and flaunt of convention, endeared him further to many blacks.

This also made him powerful political enemies. This came to a head in January, 1967 when the House Democratic Caucus stripped him of his committee chairmanship and the full House took its cue and refused to seat him. This touched off a firestorm of protest and outrage from blacks. Powell's name and cause had become a rallying cry for civil rights leaders and black activists. Two months later, the House took the rare step of kicking out one of its own members when it voted to oust him. Powell promptly took to the campus speaking circuit pleading his case, blasting variously Johnson, the Democrats, and his congressional foes. He also took swipes at mainstream civil rights organizations of which he had been at odds with over what he regarded as their cautious, go slow approach to the civil rights struggle. They returned the favor by feigning embarrassment over Powell's free-wheeling personal antics and lifestyle.

Powell was now a hot ticket speaking item on the lecture circuit and we wanted and got him. I was on the BSU speakers committee and one of my tasks was to help coordinate the in city travel arrangements of the speakers that we brought to the campus. I and another member of our speaker's committee task was to pick Powell up at his hotel, get him to the campus, and be available for anything that he needed before and after his lecture.

When we arrived at a downtown L.A. hotel where he was staying, Powell was waiting in the lobby. I had seen him many times on TV and in news photos. With his near white skin, straight hair, and chiseled features he looked like a matinee movie idol. But the Powell who greeted us effusively in the hotel lobby looked older, greyer, and seemed tired. I wasn't sure whether the battle with the House leadership over his seating had added what seemed like years to him in a matter of months or what. In the car, Powell was in a pensive mood. He seemed slightly distracted. He struck me as a man who did not make small talk.

I nervously told him that the students were really looking forward to hearing him and that there would be a full house for his speech. It was that. There was a standing room crowd in the Student Union. The sight of the students seemed to perk him up. He strode purposely to the stage. He sat with a stoic expression during the welcoming and introduction. When introduced, he bounded to the microphone to the loud and sustained applause from the students. I sat in the front row. I was as much interested in watching his mannerisms as he spoke as to what he had to say. Powell hit on most of his pet themes; his fight to regain his seat, Congress's action in ousting him, the failure of the Democrats to back him, and took swipes at civil rights leaders for being too tepid and willing to accommodate on civil rights. He also reminded the students that he was the one who had championed black power long before Carmichael shouted the words on a march in Mississippi in 1966. He reminded that he had organized and laid out a comprehensive blueprint for black political gains in 1965.

*****

Powell sounded like an aggrieved victim of political machinations, a fire eating Baptist preacher, and a master showman. He got the loudest cheer from the students when he shouted his trademark line, "Keep the faith Baby." It had a hip ring to it and the students loved it. That was the title of his book published the year before. A visibly drained Powell finally gave one more exhort to keep the faith, and then strode to his seat. Many students stood on their feet and cheered.

It was a first-class performance by a man who was used to wielding power, used to being in the spotlight, and used to expecting and hearing the cheers from adoring admirers and supporters. I quickly moved to the side of the stage. I managed to get his eye to let him know we were ready to take him back to his hotel. The speech had transformed Powell. In the car, he lit a small cheroot cigar, waved it in his hand like a wand and talked excitedly about the reaction from the students. He was clearly pleased with the reception. When we dropped him off, we were like school boys in our exuberance to tell him how much we admired and appreciated him. Powell brightened and he couldn't resist a parting "keep the faith baby" to us. We watched him as he took long looping strides into the hotel. He was all business again. He didn't look back at us.

Powell would win a special election to get his House seat back in January, 1969, and he was seated. The Supreme Court partially vindicated him in June, 1969 when it ruled that the House had acted unconstitutionally when it excluded him. But he was fined and did not get his seniority ranking back. A year later Powell's congressional tenure ended when he was defeated for reelection. Powell fled permanently to his long time safe haven in Bimini in the Bahamas.

Three years later a gravely ill Powell died at a hospital in Miami on April 4, 1972 from acute prostatitis. He was 63.

There was a revival of interest in Powell's extraordinary life and struggles in 2002 with the release of a made for TV movie on him, appropriately entitled, *Keep the Faith, Baby*. I didn't see it. I didn't need to. I had been seated in the cramped space of the back seat of an auto with this amazing, polarizing, and profoundly influential political figure that had made black political power a reality. He was a major practitioner of political maneuvering at a time when blacks were excluded or at best confined to the margins of American politics. Powell marched to his own beat in doing it. He kept the faith and showed other blacks how to do the same.

Chapter 7
Witnessing History
in One City

Chapter 7 - Witnessing History in One City

The closest I can come to describe the night and the events of June 29, 1990 were to liken it to a raging, roaring, rocking moving sea of people. This was the night that Nelson Mandela rode onto the Los Angeles Memorial Coliseum track and passed the delirious crowd that packed the Coliseum. He waved and pumped his fist and shouted to the crowd as the car with him and a small entourage of local officials slowly edged toward the stage. I entered the Coliseum through a gauntlet of vendors hawking Mandela tee shirts, African National Congress flags, and posters. There were ticket scalpers who were charging up to $20 for the event. These were the same tickets that had cost $10. The event was a fund raiser and the money would go to underwrite social and political work by his African National Congress. Los Angeles was Mandela's final stop on an eight city tour of the U.S.

Mandela's decades long battle against apartheid, a time as a gun toting, bomb planting leader of the ANC with a price on his head, his decades of brutal imprisonment and isolation was the stuff of legend. As the racist white minority regime grew more isolated and desperate and the movement against apartheid grew stronger, the name Mandela loomed larger in world stature even as he sat behind bars on Robbins Island. He was universally recognized as the titular, living symbol of that movement. He was released from prison in February, 1990. His election to the presidency in then scheduled future elections was a foregone conclusion. He would win that election in 1994 and serve one five year term as president. He would deftly guide the nation through its political birth pangs while avoiding the rancor, violence, strife, and dislocation that followed in other African nations that had gained their freedom and transitioned from white to black political rule.

But that was still in the future. I watched him take the stage at the coliseum that warm early summer night. Much of the colossal personal and political turbulence that Mandela experienced was now behind him. Mandela was a private citizen again. Yet, the delirium of the crowd at his entrance showed that his massive allure and magnetism had not diminished. As Mandela walked up the stairs to the stage, the cheers grew even louder, and the clenched fists shook even harder at each step he took up the stairs. The crowd had been pumped up by the ear piercing sounds of rock and rap music from bands that wailed away before his entrance into the Coliseum.

The organizers wisely kept the warm up introduction speeches to a minimum. The crowd was there to hear Mandela and it was in no mood to hear politicians droning on, and using the event to hog the lime light. When Mandela was announced, and took the microphone, the pandemonium hit fever pitch. He stood for a moment in the glare of the flood lights on his face, and beamed. He was ever the gracious, charming diplomat, father figure, and tactful leader as he thanked Los Angeles for its "staunch" financial support and warm, enthusiastic welcome.

He carefully avoided talking about the political struggles and the conditions in South Africa. Instead his message was more personal and generic. He punctuated it with references to the human spirit, and the sacrifice and struggle of "unsung heroes" who fought against apartheid. Then he swung curiously to the theme of drugs and addiction. He chastised the youth not to succumb to the temptation. Then he paid tribute to Hollywood and the movie stars that had been the stuff of their dreams when he and others watched their films.

This was an obvious bow to some of the celebrities such as actor Gregory Peck who had presided over an earlier talk that he gave to several thousand on the steps of the L.A. City Hall. Mandela paused before ending and gazed out into the bright lights as the crowd continued to roar with approval and adulation. He was quickly enveloped by a blanket of security agents, and police, as he walked down the steps and into the waiting car. This time it exited through a back exit gate at the Coliseum.

Barbara, and I, did not rush out when he left. The evening was too moving. I wanted to hold tightly to the feeling and bask in the moment of having seen and heard Mandela. I knew this would be the last time I and the more than 70,000 that turned out that night, would likely see Mandela. It would be his first and last visit to L.A. He had come and provided us the rare opportunity to see and hear a man whose place in history was well secure. History would position him on the high perch with such figures as King and Gandhi. They had fought, suffered, and challenged the established order. They had triumphed and would be eternally lionized for their sacrifices and struggles.

*****

I reflected on this and remembered the early discussions that I had with other students on the evil of apartheid in meetings of the BSU at Cal State L.A. in 1968. I thought about the times that a couple of black exchange students from South Africa had come to some of our meetings. We would compare the similarities of their struggle against apartheid in South Africa to the civil rights struggles in this country. The more I listened to them talk about tyrannical conditions in their country I felt a real bonding and kinship with them. One had simply to substitute Jim Crow segregation in the South for apartheid in South Africa and it seemed we were talking about the same vicious racial victimization.

The close link between both was apparent. The big difference, though, was that blacks in South Africa were the majority and whites the minority. One day the blacks would run the country. I also remembered that during those discussions Mandela's name was continually mentioned by the students. They spoke glowingly about him. He was a constant presence in their lives.

The anti-apartheid movement grew in momentum in this country during the 1980s. The principal demand was that city, and state governments, foundations and universities divest themselves of any holdings they had in corporations that did business with the apartheid regime. It was a tough fight made tougher when President Reagan staunchly resisted cutting business and military ties with the regime. Even more infuriating, some Republican conservatives lambasted Mandela as a communist, and terrorist, and placed him on the government's terrorist watch list. He stayed on that list for decades. Technically, he was banned from entering the country. His name stayed on the list even after he became the duly elected president of South Africa. Mandela persevered and lived long enough to be recognized by even some of his one-time bitterest foes as a transformative figure in history. There was little doubt of that the night I listened to him at the Coliseum.

He died in December 2013. He was 95. The night of his death I was invited to appear as a guest on *Al Jazeera* TV to discuss Mandela's legacy. I mentioned that I had heard him speak in L.A. before he became the first black elected president of South Africa. I recalled the energy and enthusiasm of the thousands that heard him that night. That feeling could only be roused by a man who had suffered much and triumphed. A man who made people feel that suffering and triumph. This was the special quality of Mandela that I'd remember most.

*****

One of those who recognized Mandela's significant place in history had hosted a reception for him at L.A. City Hall earlier in the day before his appearance at the Coliseum. In his welcoming address, Mayor Tom Bradley, hailed Mandela as a "kindred spirit" and ranked him right there with Dr. King as a powerful voice for civil rights and justice. Bradley pulled out all stops to insure that Mandela would be honored while in L.A. as the important figure that he was. Bradley was the right man to praise Mandela for having a kindred spirit with King. The same could be said for him in his own way. Bradley had not been hunted as a terrorist, jailed, beaten and tortured as Mandela. Nor had he been jailed in civil rights marches in the South as King had. However, Bradley had made a major racial breakthrough in politics that ranked high in importance.

May 27, 1969, was election night In Los Angeles. I was at the Hollywood Palladium. I had volunteered to pass out flyers, and serve as one of many poll watchers for the Bradley mayoral campaign. I joined with hundreds of others who fervently hoped that Bradley would make history by being elected the first black mayor of the nation's second largest city. His election would be another tangible by-product of the 1965 Voting Rights Bill passed in August, 1965. It was the major impetus for the quantum increase in the number of black elected officials in major and small cities across the nation. This was regarded then as the gauge of growing black political power in the country. If elected, Bradley would be the second black elected mayor of a major city in the 20th century. Two years earlier Carl Stokes had become the first when he was elected mayor of Cleveland, Ohio.

As the evening wore on the ebullient mood of the crowd, ever poised and hopeful at witnessing history, became anxious. The vote totals had begun to trickle in. Each new count showed that Bradley was slipping further and further behind incumbent two term mayor Sam Yorty. Bradley's vote slippage should not have been a total surprise. In the last weeks of the campaign, Yorty had launched a blistering, no holds barred, border line racist assault on Bradley. He painted him as left wing, and practically a communist agitator, and a black radical. This conjured up nightmarish visions among many whites of Bradley's election resulting in a takeover of City Hall by the likes of Carmichael, H. Rap Brown, and the Black Panthers.

I listened to Yorty in campaign ads on TV demean Bradley in the nauseating high nasal twang. The only thing missing was Yorty calling him the N word. Yorty would never mention Bradley by name. Instead, he'd call him "that guy," or "that fellow," spitting the words out contemptuously. Yorty got away with his not so subtle race baiting and fear mongering because of the times. The historic election came four years after the Watts riots in 1965, and a year after the summer urban riots of 1968 rocked many American cities. There were practically daily news accounts of shoot-outs between Black Panthers and the police. Carmichael and Brown were heard on newscasts saber rattling "honkies" and threatening more racial violence.

On election night, it was soon clear that Yorty's race baiting had paid off. Shortly after midnight the earlier jubilant happy mood of the crowd had turned to outright gloom and deflation. Bradley bounded on to the stage looking as stoic and unflappable as ever. His wife Ethel, and his daughters Lorraine and Phyllis, who I had graduated with from Dorsey High School, joined him. Despite the bitter loss staring him in the face and his bid to make history dashed, he cheerfully thanked those in the room for their unwavering support. He admonished us to leave since the results weren't in yet. He left us, though, with a thin sliver of hope. Later, he said that the loss was just a momentary setback, not the end of the road, and that he'd be back.

He was as good as his word. Four years later, the memories and fears of the Watts riots had receded, the Panthers had faded under FBI and police assaults, and their own internal wars, and the nation and the city had experienced a period of racial calm and peace. Yorty's race ploy fell flat. Bradley for his part had established solid ties with business, labor, and the Jewish and Latino communities. He was viewed as a coalition builder. He enjoyed the added benefit of a city that was undergoing rapid change with blacks and Latinos now forming a bigger part of the city's population.

Bradley won by a land slide. The mood this time at his election gathering stood in marked contrast to 1969. The joy was unbridled. This time it was almost a foregone conclusion that Bradley would win and win big. The night wore on and everyone in the room, cheered lustily as we watched the vote numbers in the Bradley column pile higher and higher. The election was over shortly after midnight, and Bradley had won. He now had made his claim to be another black first, and had earned a deserved place in the nation's political history.

His election was the first of what would be an unprecedented five term reign as Los Angeles city mayor. During those years Bradley was a constant whirlwind as he appeared at innumerable meetings, functions, celebrations and ground breaking ceremonies for some new development or building project. He held what he called "area days" where anyone could come in sit a spell and vent about any problem or concern they had. Bradley would be a willing listener. I would frequently see him at these events and on occasion attend one of his constituent sessions in South L.A.

Though Bradley was knocked for his bland, placid, inscrutable and stiff demeanor, on the occasions when we exchanged a few complimentary words, he would smile and give me a firm, and warm handshake. He always looked me squarely in the eye when he did. The city made a major leap forward during his first decade as mayor. There were new building developments that changed the downtown skyline. There was the start of a subway and light rail line. There were even a few new development projects in a couple of the South L.A. areas that banks, corporations and manufacturers had fled in terror and after the riots and still stood as a vast wasteland of neglect.

Bradley's political star continued to rise. And he came within a hairs breath of becoming the nation's first black governor in 1982 of California in the 20th Century. He lost by about 50,000 votes. Bradley didn't break stride and continued his break neck schedule of appearances, and events in L.A. His quest was to turn L.A. into a global showpiece city.

*****

The shiny new skyscrapers and downtown development expansion, though, couldn't mask a festering problem underneath the surface. The problem was still race and the LAPD. LAPD Chief Daryl Gates seemed to take giddy delight in antagonizing African-Americans, and in turn Bradley.

The clash between Bradley and Gates continued to escalate through the 1970s and into the 1980s. The issue was that the department by the late 1970s had become the nation's poster police agency for a racist, brutal, occupying army police force. Its head knocking tactics, massive street sweeps, and wide use of chokeholds and numerous officers involved shootings of more often than not unarmed young blacks had gained national notoriety and infamy, and Bradley struggled to rein in the department and his chief. He had the cloak of civil servant protection. And his attempts at reform were stymied and stonewalled by the L.A. city council.

By the early 1990s, race relations had deteriorated so badly that L.A. was a tender box. All it took was one spark to set it off. That spark was the LAPD beating of black motorist Rodney King in March, 1991, and the subsequent acquittal of the four officers that beat King in April 1992. In that one moment, Bradley for one of the rare times that I heard him dropped his stoic veneer, and angrily charged "Today the system failed us."

When L.A. exploded into the worst riot in 20th century America, Bradley was roundly pilloried for having inflamed blacks. He was virtually accused of being the instigator of the riots. This was nonsense. But the massive level of violence, burning, and destruction rocked Bradley back on his heels. He was the mayor and the city's second major riot in a quarter century had occurred with him at the helm in City Hall. There would be commissions, investigations and charter reforms, and the eventual ouster of Gates as a result of the civil disturbances. Yet, Bradly's political tenure was marred. He was a spent political force and he would not seek a sixth term.

In December 1998, Bradley succumbed to complications from a heart attack and a stroke. He was 80. I thought deeply how his cracking the political color bar in the nation's second biggest city had also marked my political maturing. It further spurred my deep interest in politics and an active engagement on the issues that impacted on municipal and state government in the city. The same kindred spirit that Bradley spoke of about Mandela during his 1990 visit to L.A., I also felt with Bradley.

I waited in the lengthy line of mourners with my six year old grandson, Patrick, at the public viewing of his body as he lay in state at the L.A. Convention Center. I thought hard about the history that we shared together in L.A. for two decades. I silently thanked him for what he did and the dreams that he had for the city. I thanked him for his unpretentious style, and courtly and gentlemanly approach to governance, and for his contribution to black political empowerment.

I turned to my grandson as we walked by and he stared in wide eyed wonderment at the lifeless figure in the casket and told him that he was looking at a great man. His smile told me he understood.

Chapter 8
The Fire This
Time

Chapter 8 - The Fire This Time

The on-set camera crew and sound technicians had long since departed from the sound stage at KCBS-TV in Los Angeles and the lights had dimmed. But we sat there for a short time afterward engaging in bare knuckles, heated debate. This was February, 1995. My at one moment fierce opponent and at another moment jovial associate was former Los Angeles Police Chief Daryl Gates. We were co-commentators for the station during the O.J. Simpson trial. On and off the set, we went at it on everything from the Rodney King beating, the LA riots, the LAPD's war on gang and drug violence, police misconduct and shootings, and of course, the Simpson trial.

These were the issues that tore Los Angeles for a decade before. They did more to poison relations between the LAPD and minority communities, especially African Americans, than any other. Our debates were so intense that we continued the battle of words as we walked to our cars in the parking lot. After a while this became a routine, we'd spar on the set, and continue sparring as we walked to our cars.

There were moments when Gates would sigh in exasperation that I and other critics just didn't understand what he had to face running a department that was under resourced, got little political and public support, and yet was expected to be a kinder, gentler department while battling a spiraling gang, drug and violence problem. I listened to his heart-felt pleas that he sincerely tried to make change, even reform. He repeatedly cited the number of officers that he disciplined and terminated for misconduct and other offenses, but said that his hands were tied by city officials, the police union, and the public who wanted more and tougher policing and were loath to see officers removed. He cited the community policing programs that he tried to put in place. Yet, he pleaded, nothing he did seemed to matter. He and the LAPD were still relentlessly maligned.

This was no play act or parking lot revisionism of his LAPD role to convince me that underneath the tough cop's cop exterior he was a marshmallow soft reformer. Gates passionately believed that he had done the best that he could against the odds to move the LAPD into the modern era. As we parted, I always wondered which Daryl Gates I was talking too, the maligned, misunderstood reformer, or the chief whose name was synonymous with a department that in the decade immediately preceding the King beating and the riots, had become the nation's poster police agent for a dysfunctional, brutal, racist, shoot-first, police department.

During its big, bad years, the perception, and more often than not the reality, was that the LAPD was in every sense an occupying army in South LA. Officers went where they pleased, did what they pleased and cracked heads when they pleased, all with the blind-eye acquiescence of city officials. Two massive riots, the King beating, the Rampart scandal, the Christopher and Webster commissions and a federal consent decree all made it obvious that the LAPD had to change.

Gates stood at the center of the tumultuous events that engulfed the

LAPD. He was, depending on whom one talked to, the top cop who expanded and popularized the kick-butt, SWAT teams, or the top cop who devised and expanded innovative, programs such as DARE, which served as a national police model for drug prevention and education.

Gates was well aware that the years when the LAPD carried his indelible stamp were now well past. Los Angeles city officials talked incessantly about reform and change. There was a new African-American chief. The department was now under intense federal scrutiny, and soon a consent decree mandating a total top to bottom overhaul of its policies and practices on the use of deadly force, minority hiring and promotions, and the handling of misconduct complaints. He seemed resigned to the fact time and the department had passed him by; a time when the LAPD reigned over a city that was predominantly white, with an insular city government, and where the police were roundly hailed by homeowners as heroes. That Los Angeles had rapidly faded into the past, and had morphed into one of the nation's most diverse, that demanded accountability and transparency. This meant a police force that had to change with it.

Gates, then, was truly a man of another time. His pleas and sighs of exasperation over the problems that still haunted him as we talked and walked to our cars told me much about a man who still deeply believed that he had tried to do what was best for the city, despite everything. These were the two sides of Daryl Gates that I saw as we smiled, shook hands, exchanged a laugh and walked away from each other those nights in the studio parking lot.

Yet as I walked away from Gates a harsh moment in time would always come back to me. No matter how hard I tried to see Gates as a product of, and victim of, a police force that had gained an infamous reputation for brutality and abuse, and he certainly tried hard to make his case with me, he still embodied that department. A department that history still would record as being directly responsible for igniting two of the worst riots in the nation's history, both in Los Angeles.

*****

My memory was still vivid of that hot August 11, 1965 night. I and a friend watched looters gleefully make mad dashes into the corner grocery store a half mile from my house in South L.A. Their arms bulged with liquor bottles and cigarette cartons. Suddenly, my friend shouted out as if he was speaking to an audience: "Maybe now they'll see how rotten they treat us." The "they" he meant was the white man. My friend's words were angry and bitter.

His bitter words rang in my head as I stood on the corner near my house with a small knot of neighbors and watched truckloads of grim faced National Guardsman, all young, all with bayonets fixed, and all white, as they drove by the corner of my block. This was probably their first incursion into an all-black neighborhood. The men in the guard then typically were drawn from rural and suburban areas and towns through California. They were part of the nearly 4000 National Guardsmen that patrolled the streets of South L.A. that week in

August. They enforced a tight cordon around a wide swath of South
L.A. including my block.

My friend's words did not make me feel any better on August 17, the
last night of the civil disturbance. I was awoken in the early morning
hours by the sounds of gunfire that echoed throughout my bedroom.
The war in the streets in and around my block had tragically and
graphically penetrated my home. The target of the gunfire from the
National Guard was a milkman who had failed to stop at a police
barricade.

When the smoke cleared 34 persons lay dead over 1000 were injured,
more than 600 buildings were damaged by burning and looting. The
total estimated property loss of $40 million. That's nearly $300 million
in 2014 dollars. The riots triggered a deep national soul search. There
was a highly touted commission, chaired by former CIA Director John
McCone that sought to determine the whys and wherefores of the riot.
It singled out as the causes the history of the LAPD-black community
conflict, criminal gangs, and made a nod at issues such as job, and
housing discrimination, and the total absence of health services in
Watts. It also referenced the deadly raid on the Nation of Islam
Mosque on South Broadway in April, 1962, that drew national
attention and brought Malcolm X scurrying to the city. There was also
resentment over the passage of Proposition 14, a year before in 1964.
This act struck down the Rumford Fair Housing act. It signaled the
first organized sign of the white backlash to a civil rights initiative that
would become commonplace in the next few years.

Underneath the fierce debate about why Watts happened there was a subtext of hope that the mass orgy of death and destruction that engulfed my neighborhood during the harrowing five days and nights of the Watts riots in August 1965 might improve things for blacks. Over the years, when I returned to the block I lived on during the riots, I often thought of my friend's biting yet hopeful words.

Forty years after the Watts riot, in August 2005, the reams of recommendations and proposals for change and endless promises by officials that were made to make over Watts and other decaying poor, inner city communities had remained largely unfulfilled. The streets that my friend and I were shooed down by the police and the National Guard 40 years earlier looked as if time had stood still. They were dotted with the same fast food restaurants, beauty shops, liquor stores, and mom-and-pop grocery stores. The main street near the block I lived on then was just as unkempt, pothole-ridden and trash littered. All the homes and stores in the area were all hermetically sealed with iron bars, security gates and burglar alarms.

I decided to host a 40th anniversary remembrance of the Watts riots. I organized a street corner symposium on the corner where the riot had started. The discussion would assess with the passage of the years the meaning and significance of the riots to Los Angeles and the nation. The participants were from community groups that worked in Watts, a few residents, and elected officials. They were virtually unanimous that the conditions were much the same. They agreed the government and businesses had failed miserably to keep their promises to remake Watts.

The consensus was that in the decades after the Watts riot, Watts, and the many other impoverished inner city areas of America, had largely been written off as vast empty places of violence and despair. Many banks and corporations, as well as government officials, reneged on their promises to fund and build top-notch stores, make more home and business loans, and provide massive funding for job and social service programs in such poor black, inner city areas.

Business leaders still had horrific visions of their banks and stores going up in smoke or being hopelessly plagued by criminal violence. The National Urban League in its annual State of Black America reports year after year grimly noted that blacks have lost ground in income, education, healthcare, and their treatment in the criminal justice system compared to whites. They are more likely than any other group in America to be victimized by crime and violence.

I grimaced as I read a report in 2005 by the L.A. chapter of the National Urban League and the United Way on the State of Black L.A. on the 40th anniversary of the riots. The report called the conditions in Watts and South L.A. dismal. Blacks had higher school drop-out rates, greater homelessness, died younger and in greater numbers, were more likely to be jailed and serve longer sentences, and were far and away more likely to be victims of racial hate crimes than any other group in L.A. County. The report has not been updated, but even the most cursory drive through the area showed nothing had changed.

The one significant social change in Watts, though, was the ethnic demographic shift. A half century ago, the area was predominantly black; it is now predominantly Latino, with growing numbers of Cambodian, Vietnamese and Filipino residents. The fast changing demographics have at times imploded in inter-ethnic battles between blacks and Latinos over jobs, housing and schools. There have also been deadly clashes within the L.A. county jails. Black flight also had drastically diminished black political strength in Los Angeles and statewide.

Watts is no longer the national and world symbol of American urban racial destruction, neglect and despair. However, the poverty, violence and neglect exploded in an orgy of burning, looting and destruction that I witnessed that hot August night a few blocks from my house a half century ago still had a firm place in my memory decades later. This brought me back to Gates.

*****

As I drove out of the studio parking lot the nights after sparring with Gates, my mind still kept racing about him and the tormenting history of the violence and strife that marred much of the late 20th Century relations between the LAPD and blacks. This brought back the memory of the other riot that terrifyingly defined and indelibly marked and marred those bitter relations.

It was virtually a surreal rerun of my experience of 27 years earlier. For two fateful days at the end of April and the first day of May 1992, I ducked around police cordons and barricades, and cringed in fear at the crackle of police gunfire. I choked, and gagged on and was blinded by the thick, acrid smoke that at times blotted out the sun and gave an eerie surreal *Dante's Hell* feel to Los Angeles. I watched many Los Angeles Police Department officers stand by virtually helpless and disoriented as looters gleefully made mad dashes into countless stores. Their arms bulged with everything from clothes to furniture items. I watched an armada of police from every district throughout California and the nation, National Guard units and federal troops drive past my house with stony, even scared, looks on their faces, but their guns at the ready.

I watched buildings, and stores and malls that I shopped at and frequented instantly disappear from the landscape in a wall of flames. Several friends that lived outside L.A. and were concerned about my safety implored me to leave my home in the middle of the riot area and stay with them until things blew over. I thanked them but I decided to stay put. As an award-winning journalist, I felt bound to observe and report first-hand the mass orgy of death and destruction that engulfed my South Los Angeles neighborhood during the two fateful days of the most destructive riot in U.S. history. This time the final tally of the death and destruction far exceeded the 1965 Watts riot toll. 53 people were killed, 2,000 people were injured, and over 1000 buildings were destroyed. The final tab was an estimated 1 billion dollars. In 2014 dollars the total would be nearly $1.7 billion.

The warning signs that L.A. was a powder keg were there long before the Simi Valley jury with no blacks acquitted the four LAPD cops that beat Rodney King. There was the crushingly high poverty rate in South

L.A., a spiraling crime and drug epidemic. There were neighborhoods that were among the most racially balkanized in the nation, anger over the hand slap sentence for a Korean grocer that murdered a black teenage girl in an altercation, and black-Korean tensions that had reached a boiling point. Above all, there was the angry feeling toward an LAPD widely branded as the nation's perennial poster police agency for brutality and racism.

*****

Still, it was the name Rodney King that instantly came to mind when one thought of the police-African-American community conflict and violence. This thought was again very much with me on June 17, 2012. This was less than two weeks before King's death. I was scheduled to interview him on the public stage at the annual Leimert Park Book festival in Los Angeles. I had two conflicting thoughts about the interview. One was that if the well-worn term accident of history ever applied to anyone it was King. The second was what made King such an enduring figure and a symbol. It was still the shockingly detailed video-taped beating by four white Los Angeles Police officers 21 years earlier.

It was not simply that King was the center of recent press attention with the commemoration of the twentieth anniversary of the L.A. riots. It was certainly not because he had just published a modestly successful book, *The Riot Within: My Journey from Rebellion to Redemption*. King was the near classic protean tragic figure of interest and curiosity precisely because there was so much tragedy, followed by triumph, and in the end tragedy in the way his life ended.

The tragedy was the beating. Those few brutal, savage, and violent moments, catapulted King, a marginally employed, poorly educated ex-con into a virtual global household name. It cast the spotlight on one of the nation's deepest sore spots, police abuse, brutality and misconduct against African-Americans, minorities and the poor. It turned the LAPD into the national poster symbol of a lawless, out of control, big city racist police force.

King was the most unlikely of unlikely figures to spotlight this deep national sore, to launch a painful national soul search. And, in the coming months become the trigger for the most destructive urban riot in modern US history. King, of course, was only the centerpiece for the colossal tragedy that engulfed a city and nation.

The fact remains, though, that the King beating and the subsequent riots permanently raised awareness about police abuse. I felt strongly that there was a personal triumph for King as well. When I watched him make his magnanimous statement "People, I just want to say, can we all get along? Can we get along?" at a press conference the third day of the riots, it helped stanch the violence. I watched him closely as he spoke and I was struck and moved by his utter lack of any expression of public rancor toward the LAPD and with the exception of a few minor scrapes with the law, his relatively low profile, softened some of the anger and vilification, some of it borderline racist, that King got from a wide segment of the public.

I got the news of his death while at a Sunday breakfast meeting. I felt the final tragedy was his surprising and untimely death. He was only 47. He attained a partial rehabilitation in terms of his bad guy image. He was a recognized author. His name was eternally synonymous with a number of oft-times tragic figures at the center of the many compelling events in the nation's history. It was a sad moment for me.

The ultimate irony was that these men, Daryl Gates who died on April 16, 2010, Tom Bradley, and of course, Rodney King have been publicly linked to those tumult days that I witnessed first-hand. I had seen, watched, talked to, and rubbed shoulders with them. I had marveled at how men so dissimilar in background, and their circumstance in life, could meld together in a fateful confluence of a violent history in one city. I had witnessed the flames in the city and I could never forget them.

Chapter 9
On the Hunt for
Newsmakers

Chapter 9 - On The Hunt for Newsmakers

I doubled as both a feature writer and field reporter for the *Free Press* in late 1971 and for much of 1972. This invariably meant that I'd spend the bulk of my time in the field covering news conferences, rallies, and demonstrations. That gave me an opportunity to interview and report on a number of noted personalities who came to Los Angeles for an event. In June, 1972, I was assigned to cover the Pentagon Papers trial that would be held in a downtown Los Angeles courtroom.

The defendants were Daniel Ellsberg and Anthony Russo. They were indicted by a federal grand jury on charges of espionage, theft, and conspiracy for leaking the papers to the *New York Times*.

The Pentagon Papers were a top-secret Pentagon study of U.S. government decision-making in relation to the Vietnam War,

I sat in court four days in June and July as defense and government attorneys haggled over the charges and trial procedures. Almost immediately after the trial commenced, defense attorneys stunned the court disclosing that the Nixon operatives had illegally wiretapped a conversation between either Russo or Ellsberg and their attorneys. It was a huge development. I and other reporters in the courtroom scratched our heads after the trial was ordered suspended trying to figure out what was next.

I was prepared for a long trial and figured I'd spend many days in the court listening to defense attorneys try and turn the tables and put the government on trial for its action in Vietnam. Supreme Court Justice William O. Douglass had stepped in and stayed the trial. A mistrial was declared and a new trial ordered. By then I was pulled from the coverage. I was disappointed. I badly wanted to hear the arguments and proceedings. I knew that it would be a titanic showdown over the war and America's decade long actions there. This didn't happen. The Watergate scandal had broken, and each day brought new revelations of massive law breaking by Nixon administration officials, and top level administration resignations. The government's case against Ellsberg and Russo was in shambles, and with more revelations of Nixon administration law breaking, in May, 1973, the charges against the two were dropped.

It was a busy time at the paper, and hardly a day passed without my being called out to cover an event or press conference. The largest event I covered again was held at the Los Angeles Sports Arena in November, 1971. It was an anti-war rally sponsored by the Peace Action Council. It drew more than 10,000. There were two notable differences between this rally and other anti-war rallies I had attended and reported on in the past. The first was who was there. Many of the participants were conservatively dressed, and middle aged, and they sported McGovern for president buttons. George McGovern had gained tremendous momentum in his drive for the 1972 Democratic presidential nomination running almost exclusively on one issue, and that was immediate U.S. withdrawal from Vietnam. McGovern had brought instant respectability, and drew thousands more middle-class business and professional types into the anti-war movement ranks. The other difference was the MC for the rally. It was famed actor Burt Lancaster. He brought real star power to the event. He was forceful, and animated, and kept the event moving.

He thundered from the podium that he was there to "define the problem and outline the solution." The problem was obvious and that was to get the U.S. out of Vietnam. Lancaster said the solution was putting massive pressure on Congress to "set the date" for ending the war, and any congressperson that wouldn't, Lancaster demanded, should be defeated. Lancaster's message and the tone of the rally was markedly different from the actions of student and left radical that included attacking police, firebombing buildings, and burning draft cards.

He would never have lent his name and prestige to that and a big part of the crowd that was there to see and hear him wouldn't either. Lancaster repeatedly exhorted the crowd to go to the voter registration tables that had been set up in the lobby and register to as he put it, "make your vote count." He made it official that night. Hollywood would toss its weight toward the peace movement as long as it played by the system's rules and that first and foremost as Lancaster made clear entailed voting and electoral politics. His presence there was a turning point for the anti-war movement.

I had a passing acquaintance with one of his daughters, Susan, who volunteered for a short time at KPFK while I was there. With Susan, it was a case of like father, like daughter in that both had firm liberal and progressive views on the issues and acted on the them.

Lancaster was a liberal. He and others though uneasy with the war, had largely confined their protest of it to voting and Democratic Party politics. That night anyway, Lancaster had edged to left of center and was now out in the open in his anti-war advocacy. I had been a fan of his action movies through the years, especially the 1965 World War II action movie, *the Train.* It gave me immense satisfaction to see him in person, and for him to take a public stand against the war.

*****

It was a different scene in January, 1972 at a press conference at the National Organization for Women's Center. New York Congresswoman Shirley Chisholm was in Los Angeles as part of a national campaign tour. Chisholm was on a quest to make a different sort of history. She aimed to be the first African-American woman presidential candidate from a major party, the Democratic Party. The Center was festooned with stickers "Chisholm for president," campaign hats. She sat at a table with a giant picture of her next to a paper cut-out of "Chisholm Now" on the wall.

I sat directly in the first row, and snapped madly away taking pictures. She was everything that was advertised, feisty, forceful, and no-nonsense in her answers. I was especially interested in whether she found the greatest opposition to her candidacy was because she was black or a woman. Chisholm had heard that question often. I barely got the question out when she snapped that she felt being a woman was the biggest barrier. That "middle America would be more upset" by that. She was just as direct in other questions I asked her about race, the Nixon administration's attitude toward blacks, and her stance on ending the war.

I probed her further on racism and what affect it would have on her running for president. I asked her "Are you saying that America is not as racist as it is thought to be?" Chisholm paused for a moment and fired back that she thought it was changing, and that she believed the biggest change would come from white women and white students. She offered as proof the reception that she said she got in her swing through Florida where she said there were big crowds to hear her, and a significant number of them were whites. Chisholm sat at the table after the press conference ended and greeted a steady parade of well-wishers and admirers. I saw from the expressions on the women's faces in the room that they were filled with hope and optimism that Chisholm actually could pull off the impossible and defeat the male dominated Democratic Party bosses.

I wasn't sure whether Chisholm was as confident as she posed during the press conference that she could really pull it off. I gingerly asked her before she left whether she had gotten much support from members of her own Congressional Black Caucus who had been at best lukewarm toward her candidacy. Her cryptic answer was that she had gotten support from those who "desire to give it." She didn't give any names of who that may be. I wished her well, and she smiled as she left the room surrounded by a core of National Organization for Women supporters with Chisholm for president buttons on their lapels.

Chisholm didn't and couldn't win the nomination. This was 1972 and politics then was still a rigidly controlled male affair. She well knew that. However, it was a bold, brash, and breakthrough for women in politics. In the coming decades Chisholm would be remembered for that breakthrough for women in politics. I know one thing. She had my vote. Chisholm died in 2005. She was 80.

*****

I was in a rush to get out the door of my house in June, 1972 home after I got a last minute call to cover an event that brought together a small gathering of writers and activists at the Inner City Cultural Center, which was a local black drama and arts center, near downtown Los Angeles. James Baldwin had flown in from Paris for the gathering and he would be the feature speaker. The event was a fundraiser for the Angela Davis defense effort. Davis was charged with aggravated kidnapping and first degree murder in the death of Judge Harold Haley who was killed in a hostage seizure attempt. Her case, as Newton's had been, had drawn world attention and massive support.

Baldwin was even smaller, and thinner, than he looked in the many pictures I'd seen of him. His eyes which slightly bulged, were piercing. When he spoke he stared hard at the audience. He made a few perfunctory remarks about racism, and how blacks were victimized by the prison and criminal justice system. He reserved his most pointed comments for the question and answer discussion. I was interested, though, in getting his take on the role of the black writer in the justice struggle. His thoughts on that were especially important to me, because

I considered writing my profession and, as a black writer, I was groping to assure that writing was as vital as the street activism in the struggle. I chose my words carefully, "Outline the role of the black writer in the black liberation movement" he did not hesitate, "It's very limited. He's not a politician. But he must begin F (expletive) with the people's mind. He can make the people think and have faith in themselves."

I had it. Baldwin in a terse few sentences had given me the validation that I sought. Writers had a duty to question, challenge, and expose social ills and institutions that propagate them. His words resonated with me. Baldwin was a writer, a world renowned writer. His *Notes of a Native Son, Another Country,* and *Go Tell it on the Mountain,* were required reading in innumerable college English and literature classes. And I was a writer. It was one writer, who had been there and done that with his works, namely making people think, speaking to another writer, me, who wanted to walk in his footsteps, in my own modest way. There was a reception after the Q and A, and Baldwin though looking weary, continued to be peppered with questions, that he gave short but direct answers too. Baldwin, one of America's original native sons, was back in the country that he had left in self-imposed exile for France. He was a major writer who gave his time, talent, and energy to civil rights causes, and was savagely attacked for being a black militant who befriended Malcolm X and black militants and never blanched at speaking his mind about racial injustice. He died in 1987. He was 63. He gave me a great gift that night at the Inner City Cultural Center. He made me proud to be a writer, a black writer.

Chapter 10 - O.J. Simpson through the Lens of Johnnie Cochran

The defining moment for me in the O.J. Simpson saga was not Simpson's acquittal in October, 1995, and the firestorm that it ignited nationally. It was a note I got from an associate in Johnnie Cochran's law firm. He said that Johnnie wanted me to know that he admired my comments in the case. I was one of the legion of talking head analysts during the trial, and like many of the other analysts, I was skeptical of some of Cochran's legal maneuvers.

I thought initially he badly overplayed the race card in the case, and deliberately played to the anti-police sentiments of some of the black jurors. But Cochran still went out of his way to pay me the compliment. I then paid even closer attention to his arguments and presentation in the trial. By the end of the trial he convinced me there was more than enough reasonable doubt to acquit Simpson. Most legal experts that worked with him and battled against him in major criminal and civil cases in the more than four decades of his legal career, agreed that Cochran was more than a flamboyant, race conscious, courtroom showman. He was a consummate legal professional who sought to use his prodigious legal talent to defend the rights of the poor and the dispossessed. Cochran set a lofty standard for advocacy law that influenced a generation of criminal and public advocacy attorneys.

A few months after the close of the Simpson trial, I called Cochran's law office to set up an interview with him on my KPFK radio talk show. A day later Cochran returned the call and left a message apologizing that he would not be available at the time scheduled. But he left it open for an interview at another time. I was disappointed but I appreciated that he took the time to return my call and acknowledge my request. The personal touch was enough salve for me.

The complimentary note I got from him was not the first time that I had had an interaction with him. Cochran had crossed my personal radar scope three decades before Simpson's acquittal. In the spring of 1966, I sat riveted to the TV watching this then 28 year old young flamboyant, thin, ball of energy, black attorney give a spellbinding performance in the televised coroner's inquest into the LAPD slaying of Leonard Deadwyler in May, 1966. The inquest took place in a downtown Los Angeles courtroom. Deadwyler was an unarmed black motorist who was shot by an LAPD officer while taking his pregnant wife to the hospital. He was the latest in the legion of blacks that had been shot by the LAPD under dubious circumstances. The killing attracted national attention in that it came months after the Watts riot and race relations in Los Angeles and across the nation were at the flashpoint.

In the inquest, Cochran focused public attention on the LAPD's policies and practices. His aim was to put the LAPD on trial. The cameras honed in on Cochran who due to the then arcane rules of procedure in coroner's inquests was forbidden to pose questions directly to the court. There ensued the ludicrous almost comical scene of Cochran whispering into the ear of the deputy district attorney a series of probing and challenging questions about Deadwyler's death. I watched as the DA repeated over and over again: "Mr. Cochran wants to know ..." Cochran's whisper was repeatedly caught on camera. That day a legal star was born. Cochran's skill at fingering police abuse heightened public awareness of racism, police violence, and the need for major reforms in police practices.

This was the first time that I had seen a black attorney in a court of law. The televising of the Deadwyler inquest enhanced the drama and the importance of the case. Years later, I attended a symposium in which Cochran spoke to a confab of black law students. He discussed cases he had been involved with and his law practice. He interspersed his talk with words of encouragement for young blacks who wanted to pursue a career in law. He had the audience in stitches with his wry humor and anecdotes. He was not just a smart guy, and one of America's top legal guns, he was also down to earth and funny.

*****

Cochran was deeply influenced by the monumental legal battles that civil rights notables Charles Houston and Thurgood Marshall fought against segregation and police violence in the 1940s and 1950s. Cochran publicly credited them with inspiring him to champion civil rights causes in the courtroom. Cochran stamped his biggest imprint on the volatile issue of police abuse. Over the years, his fame and reputation grew, and he got richer in the process. Yet, he still continued to battle police abuse. He waged a thirty year battle to free

Black Panther Elmer Geronimo Pratt who was falsely convicted of the robbery of a couple on a Santa Monica tennis court and the murder of Caroline Olson during that robbery in 1968. Cochran exposed how the government used paid agents to frame black militants and disrupt black organizations.

Cochran repeatedly said the Pratt case and victory was a key moment in his career. He continued to press to have Pratt's conviction overturned. He filed innumerable appeals and writs in state and federal courts to overturn the conviction and get a new trial. In 1997, Pratt's conviction was overturned and he was released. The case was an extension of Cochran's relentless fight for justice in the courts.

I took a keen interest in the Pratt case for reasons that went beyond just the issue of injustice to him. I was convinced Pratt was innocent. A year after he was imprisoned in 1972, he had written me a deeply personal letter from San Quentin in 1972. He laid out in precise detail a chronology of where he was at the time he was alleged to have committed the robbery and murder. He was in a meeting in Northern California at the time of the crime. The FBI through wiretaps and informants knew that but suppressed that crucial information. This supported in every detail the facts that Cochran later used as the basis of his many appeals to win Pratt's release.

*****

I admired, respected, and applauded Cochran's impeccable legal skills and dogged commitment to take cases that promised not just big monetary rewards, but in some way sought to attain social and legal justice. His reputation for that was such that there was little doubt that the instant Simpson was arrested and charged with the double murder, Cochran would be involved in the case. He was regarded then simply as one of the best criminal trial attorneys in the nation. And Simpson would need the best. He was charged with a capital crime and could face the death penalty.

The case would be another milestone for Cochran and it would be a defining moment for me too. In January, 1995, KCBS-TV hired me to join a team of legal commentators, experts, and commentators to do an analysis of the key legal and social issues each day's court proceeding raised. This insured that I would have a chance to watch Cochran each day through the twists and turns of a trial that would be a global phenomenon, and the subject of endless impassioned fury, anger, debate and controversy. The man that Cochran and his top notch legal team would try to keep off death row was more than a celebrated football great, TV pitchman, and actor. He had been praised and admired by many as an African-American notable who eschewed racial politics and protest, and rarely if ever made any comment about civil rights issues.

The one time I did see and talk with Simpson was in the spring, 1969 at a fraternity party near the USC campus. He was a senior at USC then. He had won the Heisman Trophy in 1968 and was everyone's All-American. Even then, he was a household name in Los Angeles and increasingly the nation. The party was packed. The liquor was flowing and everyone was having a good time. Simpson, and his first wife Marguerite, were sitting in a room adjacent to the kitchen, away from everyone. They were talking quietly. I paused for a moment in the kitchen and watched them. Party goers would saunter into the room to shake his hand and make small talk.

Some asked for an autograph. I resisted as long as I could. Finally I walked in, shook his hand, made small talk about football, and wished him well. Simpson was gracious and polite. He smiled and acknowledged the glad handers. I could sense, though, that he wanted to maintain his distance. He was conscious of his image and status. There was an invisible line he drew between himself and the public. He existed in a rarified world that few could ever enter. This was the world of the budding superstar, an All American hero athlete. He seemed even then a man consigned to a life of splendid, self-imposed isolation.

He was everything that Cochran wasn't. Cochran had that innate earthy and refreshing manner and was engaging with people. He loved the cars, jewelry, and fine living. Still, he retained that down home quality that was magnetic and he possessed an irresistible charm and graciousness.

*****

The Simpson case was yet another example to Cochran of how a black defendant, even a rich black celebrity defendant such as Simpson, could be victimized by the criminal justice. The issues again were racism, and police misconduct.

Cochran did not, as I had earlier mistakenly believed, play on race to manipulate the jurors and get Simpson off. He meticulously picked apart the flaws, contradictions and inconsistencies in the prosecution's case. The case was won on the evidence or lack thereof, and not race, and Cochran would take much heat for his skill and Simpson win. This was plainly evident to me in June 2014, which marked the twentieth anniversary of Simpson's arrest for the murders. Simpson had just filed a 102 page petition pleading with the Nevada Supreme Court to grant him a new trial on his robbery, kidnapping and weapons conviction in 2008. Simpson was serving a nine to 33 year sentence.

*****

Simpson's petition and the twenty year passage of the murders sparked a brief rash of speculation over whether he had a legal leg left to stand on. Simpson had already been turned down by Nevada courts in a request for a new trial and his one half-hearted appeal to President Obama last January for clemency was more a laugh line than a serious hope that Obama would even acknowledge the appeal. His latest court appeal would likely go nowhere and Simpson would almost certainly serve every minute of the minimum of his sentence.

I knew when I watched Simpson shackled in court that would satisfy the court of law. But it would never totally satisfy many in the court of public opinion. The reason is simple. Simpson's acquittal on the double murder charges nineteen years ago still stuck in the craw of much of America. The bloggers and legal pundits who had anything to say about Simpson's petition for a new trial spent little time talking about that and nearly all their time talking about the murders, and how a murderer supposedly gamed the system and skipped away scot free. If Simpson stayed alive long enough to serve every day of his sentence he was slapped with that would not be good enough for many.

Even then more than a few commentators and legal analysts assessed Simpson's dim chances of getting a new trial, reminded that it was Cochran who bore culpability in letting a double murderer evade justice. They echoed what much of the public had repeatedly said in the years after Simpson's acquittal. Cochran would spend those years in speeches, two autobiographies, and several articles explaining his action in the case.

In the years after the Simpson acquittal I would occasionally see Cochran at different functions, and each time he did not duck the thorny issues in the Pratt, Simpson and the other police abuse cases that he was involved in during his career. The audiences as was the case nearly two decades earlier when I first heard him speak always sat in rapt attention, and when he finished they would leap to their feet in sustained applause to show their deep appreciation and admiration for his work.

In his final years, Cochran railed at the Bush administration for trampling on civil rights in the war on terrorism. In one of his last major speeches at the mostly white, upper crust Commonwealth Club in Los Angeles in 2002, Cochran blasted then Attorney General John Ashcroft for eroding civil rights and warned, "They're not going to say later, hey, you know, we're just taking those for a little while until we work this little problem out." Cochran understood that civil rights were not a "little problem" but were precious commodities that had to be safeguarded at all costs, and that the Bush administration imperiled those rights.

Cochran largely disappeared from public view after 2002. He was battling the brain cancer that would ultimately claim his life in March, 2005. He was 67. When his death was announced I thought not of the dapper, media savvy, legal wizard. I didn't think of the man who was credited and vilified for freeing Simpson. Nor did I think of the acclaim he got for the long list of celebrity clients such as Michael Jackson he represented. I thought of the man who took the time to respond graciously to my invitation to guest on my radio show. I thought of the Cochran who sent me a solicitous note of thanks for my commentary during the Simpson trial. This is the Johnnie Cochran that I knew and admired. I would remember him for much more than O.J.

Chapter 11 - It Was More Than a Game

I didn't know much about basketball the year before I started my freshmen year at Mt Carmel High School in Chicago in 1960. There were two names, though, that I did hear repeatedly when the game was mentioned. The first was the Harlem Globetrotters. The other was Wilt Chamberlain. The Globetrotters were a home grown product of black Chicago. The Globbies as they were affectionately called were founded in 1926 and played their first games at the famed Savoy Ballroom on Chicago's South Side. They had gone from there to become a virtual institution in black America. They were regarded for a time as black America's team. Then later the Globbies became a global attraction. Despite their fame, what didn't change was that when they played in Chicago, the seats were filled. Their slapstick court antics always had fans in stitches in their seats and the aisles.

It was not just their buffoonery, clowning, and ribald play, which at times was roundly criticized by some black commentators as promoting the worst stereotypes of blacks as clown, coons and toms. The Globbies were embraced because these were black men who actually drubbed their white prop straight men, and provided fun and merriment in doing it. This gave us special satisfaction.

In 1958 Chamberlain had joined the Globetrotters for a year before entering the NBA. He had by far become the Globbies biggest draw. He had bagged the largest contract ever paid to a Globetrotter. That evening that I sat in the stands at the Chicago Stadium with my father at the team's annual appearance in Chicago. Chamberlain didn't disappoint. He brought the house down with the Globbie's trademark end of the game antic. One of the Globetrotter guards would jump up on Chamberlain's shoulders and throw down a windmill rim rattling dunk. Chamberlain would go on to rewrite the record book in the NBA and change the game forever, dominating the game like no other big man had then done or done since. He would stir some controversy along the way with his public boasts of his sexual conquests, and his endorsement of Richard Nixon in the 1968 presidential campaign.

That meant little to me. Chamberlain was a proud, independent, do it my way black man, and that resonated with me. I would occasionally see him at *Dulan's Soul Food* restaurant in L.A.'s Marina Del Rey. He was always cordial when I smiled and nodded at him. The memory of Chamberlain's days with the Globetrotters from the time that I saw him in Chicago remained strong. I closely followed his NBA career. When he retired, he quickly took up the sport that he had tinkered with during his basketball days. That was volleyball. He had become a founder of the International Volleyball Association. He sponsored, coached and become a part time player with the Orange County Stars in 1977 and played their matches in Orange County, California. I had scant interest in the sport. But Chamberlain's identification with the sport had made it a big draw and that interested me too. I wanted to see him play. I drove with my daughter to Orange County one evening in early 1978 to see him.

During the match, he paced the sidelines gesturing and exhorting his players. When he entered the game, the crowd cheered wildly every time he would make a swooping return slam of an offensive serve. He was still bigger than life to the fans. That evening he played the role of coach and motivator for the players to the hilt. Chamberlain was as passionate about the sport as he had been about basketball. And it showed. Afterward I nudged my daughter to join with the knot of other fans to get his autograph. Chamberlain was very cordial. He signed her program, and gave her a faint smile. I thanked him, and quickly departed. Chamberlain dabbled for a time with films, forming his own production company and coaching track. However, he still kept a close eye on the sport that had made him a major name, and was just as outspoken in criticizing the big salaries that the stars of the 1980s and 1990s were getting. With him, it seemed less jealousy than simply recognizing what he was and should have been worth during his days when he rewrote the record books.

That was simply Chamberlain being Chamberlain; as always, his own man. He died in October 1999. He was 63. I thought about the Globetrotter game in Chicago in 1958 and how I thrilled at watching him and later how I got the same feeling watching him on the volleyball court decades later. It was a refreshing confirmation for me that he was and would always be bigger than his sport.

*****

Chamberlain's career attained near mythic proportions. However, there was one other sports figure that could make an even bigger claim to the title of legend. In April 1967 Muhammad Ali refused induction into the army. That made it official. He was now the American government and boxing's biggest pariah. His conversion to the Nation of Islam, his friendship with Malcolm X, his outspoken Muslim preachments on black pride and empowerment had made him a controversial figure. Now Ali capped that with his refusal to be inducted and his denunciation of the Vietnam War.

Ali became a much sought after speaker at anti-war protests, rallies and on college campuses after he took his stance against the draft and the war. In the spring 1968, the Black Student Union of which I was Vice President at Cal State L.A. eagerly agreed to be one of the sponsors of Ali's talk on the campus. From the time that I sat at the Los Angeles Sports Arena in February 1964 with my father and watched a young, brash, Ali, stun Sonny Liston in the 7th round with a TKO win and capture the heavyweight boxing title, Ali was bigger than his sport to me.

Now four years later he was coming to speak at our school. I, and a small entourage of BSU members, met him in the parking lot. As he got out of the car, I spontaneously extended my hand and he grabbed it in a firm handshake and said "my brother." We trailed behind his stone faced, vigilant entourage of Nation of Islam bodyguards as he strode to the Student Union auditorium. Along the way Ali basked in the adulation from the students, who pushed and shoved and jostled to see and touch him. Occasionally he would engage in light hearted banter with the students. He'd mug with one of the students in a playful boxing stance. His talk by then was mostly the stock, one liners about an unjust war, and the draft. He sprinkled his talk with constant and obligatory praise of NOI leader Elijah Muhammad. He brought the house down with his boasts that he was still the biggest, baddest and prettiest in the world.

He departed the building, but continued to banter with the students. They jostled to get close to touch him and pat him on the back, and shout encouragement. Our very feeble attempt to be his campus protectors had long since crumbled in the mania, excitement and crush of students hemming him in as he walked back to the parking lot. In an instant Ali was gone, but the excitement over his appearance wasn't. It would be the talk of the campus and BSU meetings for the next couple of weeks.

This was not the first time I thought I'd play a small role as one of Ali's "protectors" in a public venue. A year before his Cal. State L.A. speech, in June 1967, I drove to Century City to participate in what was then billed as the largest anti-Vietnam war protest in the city. The immediate target was Lyndon Johnson who was scheduled to speak at the Century Plaza Hotel. Ali was one of the featured speakers. The march gained national infamy when club wielding LAPD officers waded into the marchers, bloodying many of them. I had retreated to a park near the hotel where I knew that Ali had to pass through to get to one of the parking lots.

There was panic and chaos. Ali was being hustled across the grass area. I quickly fell in as part of his impromptu security line. We joined hands and surrounded him and moved him as if a unit across the field.

Suddenly in the midst of the chaos, Ali stopped for a few moments as I and several others pulled out our draft cards and shoved them at him. He took mine and the others and signed his name on them. I waved the card triumphantly in the air as if I had just scored a knockout over Sonny Liston. The triumph though was my act of defiance and protest over the war that I had vowed I would not fight in.

Ali finally won his bout against the government when the Supreme Court overturned his conviction in June 1971. Three months earlier, Ali had fought undefeated heavyweight champ Joe Frazier at Madison Square Garden. The match was one of the most anticipated sporting events in ages. It was not a boxing match but a major news event. I, and many others, felt that we had died that night when Ali whom we fervently believed was invincible went down to the canvas from a crushing left hook by Frazier.

His loss was my loss. I would see all of his fights in theaters (this was the era before pay TV). The three ring wars with Frazier and others. One which had special significance was his bout with Ken Norton. In their first fight of which there would be three, Norton gave Ali all he could handle. He became only the second man to beat him in 1973 and broke his jaw in the fight. There was a personal connect for me with Norton. I met him at a backyard barbecue at my cousin, Shelly Daniels, house in Altadena in 1971 a couple of years before the Ali fights. He was gentle, and playful, and came off as just a regular guy. I liked him. He would always be remembered, though, as the man who broke Ali's jaw in the ring. Norton died in 2013. He was 70. In every remembrance of and tribute to him, there was always mention made that Norton had broken Ali's jaw in the ring.

In a backdoor way, that mention spoke of Ali's towering importance in that a life and the boxing career of one of his opponents, Ken Norton, could be a measure of his importance. This wasn't a stretch. The Ali that twice shook my hand, warmly greeted me, and signed my draft card it seemed had been so much a part of my life for so long. Even as he battled the Parkinson's disease that had reduced him to a shell of his former self, he was still to me and millions of others worldwide simply "the greatest."

*****

Ali and Chamberlain's era marked the pinnacle of the socially conscious black athlete. Jim Brown, Kareem Abdul Jabbar, Bill Russell, Curt Flood, Hank Aaron, and Tommy Smith and John Carlos, with their black power protest at the 1968 Mexico City Olympic games, did more than speak out against racial injustice in sport and society, they also took action. They backed the 1968 Olympic boycott, formed black business development organizations and put forth proposals for black economic empowerment. I saw them frequently on the playing field, basketball court, baseball diamond and at track meets. I had interviewed, and appeared on a TV show with Jim Brown.

The one athlete that I developed an especially close working relationship with during that period was UCLA and pro basketball great Walt Hazzard. He was not on the A list of media outspoken black athletes. But he was every bit the icon of conscience as Ali was and every bit as impassioned about the black struggle. Hazzard was generally recognized as the one player who above all was responsible for the launch of the NCAA record setting string of championships that UCLA snared under the masterful coaching of John Wooden. He was the spark for the first one in 1964.

He was the prototypical playmaking, penetrating point guard. He went on to rack up winning years as a basketball coach at Compton College and briefly took over the coaching reins at UCLA in the 1980s.

In the mid-1970s, Hazzard converted to Islam and took the adopted name of Mahdi Abdul Rahman. In the fall of 1975, I had a sports program called "Out of Bounds" on KPFK. The first person I reached out to consider being an occasional guest co-host on the show was Rahman. On the shows, we talked sports, but not just scores, highlights, and personalities. We talked about the politics of sport. The issue always came back to the exploitation of the black athlete at colleges with their abysmal graduation rates and in the pros where they were summarily put out to pasture when their always short lived playing days were over.

Rahman often came to the station with his Koran and several other religious tracts. In between the show breaks, he would take a quick glance at a passage he had highlighted. We did our last broadcast together in the spring of 1976, and a month later the show was cancelled. I would occasionally call him to get his take on some controversy involving a sports figure, and he would give me his usual blunt and insightful observation. Even after he suffered a stroke that left him partially paralyzed, Rahman stayed close to the game he still loved. I applauded Lakers owner Jerry Buss who announced shortly after Rahman's illness became known that he would keep him on the team's payroll as long as he owned the team. Buss was as good as his word. He remained a member of the team until his death in 2011. He was 69.

Rahman was not just a star basketball player. He was a man who had a deep awareness of the plight of many black athletes in and out of their sport. He was never afraid to speak his mind about their plight. He was willing to use his name and status as a name black athlete to draw public attention to racial injustices. He showed that time and again with me. He earned my lasting respect and admiration.

******

As a kid growing up on Chicago's South Side in the 1950s I loved baseball. But most blacks then didn't love the Chicago Cubs. There were two reasons for that. The Cubs played at Wrigley field on Chicago's North Side and blacks almost literally took their lives in their hand walking or driving though the lily white, rabidly hostile neighborhoods around the ball park. The other was that most blacks then lived on Chicago's South Side. They adored the Chicago White Sox who played at Comiskey Park on the South Side.

Many remembered that five years before Jackie Robinson crashed through the color bar in baseball in 1947 with the Dodgers, the

Chicago White Sox gave him a look see tryout in 1942. When the Sox were away team owners rented the stadium out to Negro League teams and the biggest game for the Negro Leagues was the East-West Classic all-star game held each summer at Comiskey. My father and other blacks regularly jammed the park to watch some of the era's top baseball talent. Nearly all of whom in the early to mid-1950s still had almost no chance to crack the color bar that had morphed from the rigid barrier before Robinson broke it in 1947 to a gentleman's arrangement among the owners to clamp a tight quota on the number of blacks that each team could have on their roster at any one time.

Despite my disdain for the Cubs, the name that I and every black baseball fan in Chicago knew was Ernie Banks. I closely followed Banks exploits. I'd listen to Cubs games on the radio. When the announcer said "And now Banks is stepping to the plate" I got a thrill of pride and anticipation that with that easy almost nonchalant trademark batting style of his with the right elbow cocked high, he would smack one out of the park. When he did I screamed with delight. The avalanche of accolades, tributes to, and remembrances of Banks, on his passing made the obligatory gush that he was a great player and a model of decorum and civility. The undertone to this is that Banks, unlike Robinson, was a great guy because he never uttered a peep about racial bias within and without baseball. This supposedly enhanced his status as a paragon of greatness. This deliberately distorts and ignores what Banks said and had to face when he broke in with the Cubs in 1953.

Banks lived on Chicago's South Side not far from where I lived. He often commuted to Cubs home games on the el train. He had no choice. Though he was the biggest name and biggest draw the Cubs had, he could not buy a home or rent an apartment in the neighborhood surrounding Wrigley Field. I remember my father and other blacks talking about how Banks privately would complain that few blacks ever came to Wrigley field for Cubs games. Years after he hung up his glove in 1971, he opened up and expressed his disappointment at the invisible racial barrier for Cubs games, "I lived with a lot of schoolteachers and bankers, and they never came to Wrigley."

Banks tried to do something about that. He cajoled John Johnson, the publisher of *Ebony* and *Jet*, to buy Cubs season tickets one year. A decade after his debut with the Cubs, Johnson became reportedly the Cubs' first African-American season-ticket holder. It was all for naught. Johnson didn't use them and Banks told why, "He called me and said, 'Ernie, I gotta cancel my tickets. I can't get nobody to go with me!'"

Banks did not turn a blind eye to the Cubs unstated quota system for black players in the 1950s. He acknowledged that the Cubs would quickly trade away young black players. He flatly attributed the reluctance of blacks to come to Cubs games to the lack of black players on the team.

Even though we didn't go to Cubs games, Banks deeply appreciated the support he got from the blacks on Chicago's South Side especially in the neighborhood where he and I lived. He said so, "Very few blacks came to Wrigley Field at that time and, in my own community, people were really proud of me. They assisted me, made sure I got to bed on time, congratulated me. ... It wasn't like I was a star or a hero. It was like I was taken in, like a family. They would come and watch my kids, wash my car, invite me to dinner."

I was not a fan of the Cubs. I was a fan of Banks. I cherished him for his phenomenal baseball skills, grace, warmth and dignity. He was a sports role model for me and other young blacks in Chicago at a time when we desperately needed them in the Big Leagues. He was a man who never forgot that his achievements on and off the field meant so much to us. That's the other Mr. Cub I'll always remember.

*****

It was April 1997 I waited with a small knot of other admirers and well-wishers near the lectern in the UCLA Student Union where she had just said a few brief words about her husband to the audience of several hundred that had filled one of the conference rooms. Rachel Robinson was at UCLA to accept an award from the school on behalf of her late husband Jackie Robinson. She was also there to help promote the recently published authorized, definitive biography on Robinson, *Jackie Robinson*, by noted historian Arnold Rampersad. He also spoke. Rachel displayed a warm glow and with her smooth, and pristine skin. She looked more youthful than ever on the podium. It was as if time had stopped with her. She spoke with the same class and supreme dignity that she and Jackie continually displayed in the face of the many adversities they confronted through the years. She thanked the chancellor, faculty and staff members who had turned out for the event.

I had hoped to set up a time during her visit for an in studio interview on my weekly Tuesday Night Live show on KPFK. However, I was told that due to time constraints Rachel would not be able to come to the station. But I could do a brief interview with her by phone. It would be live. I considered that a rare honor. In speaking with her, it was almost as if I was talking to Jackie. I did not have much interest in baseball growing up in Chicago in the 1950s so I had never seen Robinson play when the Dodgers came to town to play the Cubs. But in high school, I had seen his biopic *The Jackie Robinson Story* . Untrained in acting, Robinson played himself and I thought he did a credible job in telling his story up until 1950 when the film was made. A young, up and coming actress, Ruby Dee, played Rachel in the film.

Still, I had seen Jackie numerous times interviewed on TV, and at press conferences sitting next to Dr. King as the civil rights movement heated up in the 1960s. Robinson was in continual demand as a prime fundraiser and celebrity attraction for King and the NAACP. It seemed wherever there was a civil rights flare up, Robinson was there.

After Robinson's death in October, 1972, the task fell to Rachel as his wife, but more importantly, as a committed activist, and compatriot in the civil rights struggle to promote his legacy. To that end, she established the Jackie Robinson Foundation to give scholarships to minority youths for higher education, as well as preserving Robinson's name and legacy. In the early years of its establishment, Rachel was tireless in her work with the foundation.

The publication of the seminal work on Robinson by Rampersad gave a complete picture of the full measure of the paramount personal and professional challenges that Robinson faced within and without baseball and how he dealt with them. I had written extensively about those challenges in several articles assessing Robinson's struggles on the 50th anniversary of his breaking the color line in baseball. I wrote that on April 15, 2007, then President Bill Clinton stood at second base at New York's Shea Stadium with Rachel Robinson during a nationally televised game between the Los Angeles Dodgers and the New York Mets.

He honored the 50th anniversary of Robinson smashing baseball's color barrier. Clinton saluted Robinson's memory, and told the world how his monumental accomplishment permanently enriched American sports and society. Clinton was right.

Yet when Robinson nervously stood at second base in his first game in the majors he was "uneasy" and far less hopeful that his feat would change American attitudes toward blacks. Twenty-five years after that historic day in 1947 Robinson's unease became bitter doubts. In his autobiography, "*I Never Had it Made*," he unapologetically declared: "I cannot stand and sing the anthem. I cannot salute the flag. I know that I am a black man in a white world. I never had it made."

During the 1997 baseball season there were loads of romanticized testimonials and speeches about Robinson's story in baseball. But there wouldn't be much said about his story outside of baseball. This was the other story that Robinson told in his autobiography and in letters and columns in the *New York Post* and the *Amsterdam News* in the 1960s. The one that I remembered was that in 1972 shortly before his death Robinson had refused to attend an old-timers game and accused baseball owners of running "a big selfish business" for refusing to hire blacks as managers, coaches and front-offices executives. Robinson was then greatly disappointed at that and was not afraid to say it. The old fire against what he perceived as discrimination and injustice had not been doused.

Rachel was still very much alive and she was determined to keep the remembrance of his legacy alive. In her calm, deliberative, almost matter of fact manner, in the radio interview, she talked with me about the foundation and its work. She said that she thought Jackie would be disappointed that blacks still had not attained more parity in front office and coaching positions in baseball and that he would be just as incensed over discrimination in other areas of American life.

Despite all that he went through and the many disappointments and periods of disillusionment he experienced, Rachel reiterated that Jackie had remained an optimist about life and the progress that the country had made and could make. She continually referred to Rampersad's book, and how pleased she was that it had given such a revealing picture of the fine details of Jackie's life that often escaped the public in the intense glare of the media light he was under for so many years.

Rachel came back to UCLA in 2009 to receive the UCLA chancellor's award from UCLA Chancellor **Gene Block** for her lifetime achievements. The UCLA Medal is the university's highest honor and was created to "honor those individuals who have made extraordinary and distinguished contributions to their professions, to higher education, to our society, and to the people of UCLA." The medal was awarded to her, not Jackie, for her accomplishments. This was recognition that Rachel was more than Jackie Robinson's wife. She was a major force in her own right. I called her a day after to congratulate her. I didn't speak to her directly but left a message thanking her for being there for Jackie and being here for us.

The Foundation again made brief news in August 2013 when the statue of Jackie Robinson that stands outside Brooklyn's minor league baseball office was defaced with the scrawl "Heil Hitler." Police investigated it as a racial hate crime, and the Foundation announced that a reward fund swelled to $50,000 had been put up for information leading to the apprehension of the culprits. Four decades after his death, the defacing of the statue seemed to typify how decades after Robinson cracked the color bar in baseball, he was still a controversial figure to some.

Robinson got the break of the century when he was chosen by Dodger owner Branch Rickey in 1947 to smash the color barrier. He was courted by politicians, showered with personal honors and attained a measure of financial success. At the end of his life he realized that many blacks had continued to lose ground: "I can't believe that I have it made while so many of my black brothers and sisters are hungry, inadequately housed, insufficiently clothed, denied their dignity, live in slums or barely exist on welfare."

In her own quiet, supremely dignified way, Rachel said pretty much the same thing to me in the interview. In speaking for Jackie she spoke for herself as well.

Chapter 12
Five Others I Saw

Chapter 12 - Five Others Who Made their Mark

There were five others who made their mark on the events of the last four decades. They had the good fortune to see the dawn of the 21st Century. They passed. The legacy they left respectively in music, the arts, the media, and with one just by attaining a record for longevity, didn't. I had the equally good fortune to witness each one of them fashion their legacy bit by bit.

The Gil Scott-Heron that showed up at KPFK's studios for a scheduled interview with me in the mid-1970s was not at all like the man I expected. The Heron I expected was a hard edged, posturing, rhetoric spouting black militant. Instead Gil was soft spoken, had an easy laugh, and was witty.

The interview was less an interview about his music and his album *Winter in America,* released in 1974, than his probing me about how conditions were for blacks in the city, police problems, and the organizations fighting for change. Heron was in Los Angeles on a performance and promotional tour for the album. I even forgot for a moment that I was talking to one of the premier musical artists of the day. I felt I was discussing the political and social issues of the day with a social scientist.

Nearly four decades later, it seemed and sounded odd to read and hear the tributes and remembrances of Heron after his **death** that exclusively focused on two things. One was his fast paced, hard edged, take no prisoners signature single "The Revolution Will Not Be

Televised." The other was to label him "the Godfather of Rap." Neither of these did justice to Heron. The spoken word "Revolution" was hardly the first or the hardest hitting musical homage to the spirit of black radicalism of the times.

In fact, by the time "Revolution" hit the airwaves in the early 1970s, black singers, jazz musicians, and spoken word poets had been pouring out incendiary black radical lyrics, sounds, and poetry for several years. The rap cadences were pronounced in many of their works. In the decades before the 1960s, legions of black jazz, bee bop, and blues singers "rapped", scatted, and hooped in their songs.

The irony is that Heron took great pains to distance himself from many of the rap artists that purportedly were influenced by him. He decried their resort to shock, demeaning, and degrading lyrics and words, and their lust for the bling and opulence, at the expense of socially grounded and edgy lyrics that blasted oppression and injustice.

Heron's true importance and legacy was that he was the textbook liberated spirit, a musical social and political griot who refused to tone down or compromise his scathing political attacks on the establishment. Heron didn't just hector, pick at and tweak the establishment to protest racism and the struggles against injustice. He was a thought provoking musical educator. And nothing was off limits. He railed at the pardon of Richard Nixon on "We Beg Your Pardon." He lashed out at government lies, deceit and corruption in the Watergate scandal on ""H2O Gate Blues."

He was outraged at the **murder** of Jose Campos Torres, an army vet murdered by two Houston police officers, on "Jose Campos Torres." He took a shot at the spending on **space** exploration with so many problems on Earth on "Space Shuttle." He mocked America's bicentennial hoopla in 1976 on "Bicentennial Blues." He lambasted prison abuses following the Attica prison uprising on "The Prisoner."

His landmark album *Winter in America* was both a grim, bitter, look at racial and political oppression in America and optimistic call for the forces of hope and change to renew the struggle against it. His equally signature song *From South Africa to South Carolina* forcefully and brilliantly linked the struggles of Africans and African-Americans against apartheid, racism, colonialism and neo-colonialism. To Heron, the struggles were one and the same. The oppressor was one and the same, and those struggling against it shared a common bond.

The other mark of Heron's genius was that he did not just wage a bitter lyrical battle against the purveyors of oppression. He did it with style, wit and humor. There was a sort of impishness in his satirizing and poking fun at everyone from Nixon to the mainstream civil rights leaders of the day.

The humor in his lyrics was so contagious that even the Urban League's Whitney Young would have had to chuckle at this line in the "Revolution" and "There will be no slow motion or still life of Whitney Young being run out of Harlem on a rail with a brand new process." Or NAACP's Roy Wilkins might have smiled at this line in "Revolution," "There will be no still life of Roy Wilkins strolling through Watts in a red, green and black liberation jump suit that he had been saving for just the proper occasion." Heron's thunderbolts against oppression were rough, but one never got the sense that there was any mean-spiritedness in them.

In the studio with me, he smiled and laughed so easily and so often during our conversation. There was no way I could see him as anything other than an easy going, fun loving, but at the same time, serious observer of the social scene.

He died in May 2011. He was 62. In later years, he battled his own demons, drug addiction, and incarceration, and for a long stretch he disappeared from the musical scene. He never forgot his mission. It was simple. He wanted to tell a story of injustice and those who waged that struggle against injustice. He had the great gift to tell that story with passion, toughness, beauty and humor. We owe him thanks for sharing that gift with us. He certainly shared it with me that day at KPFK. That indeed can't be televised.

*****

The accolades and tributes poured in fast and furious when the news hit that the host of CBS's flagship *60 Minutes* had passed in November 2006. He was 65. What struck me about most of them was that they read and sounded like canned platitudes about Ed Bradley. They pretty much followed the same script. They justly lauded Bradley's colossal news accomplishments, listed the piles of awards he received, and hailed him for the giant role he played as mentor, role model and inspirational father figure to successive waves of black journalists and newspersons. President Bush, for instance, expressed the obligatory sadness over Bradley's death, and gave the equally obligatory tout of him as one of the most accomplished journalists of our times.

Bush and the others that paid tribute to him only reaffirmed Bradley as a news icon. It didn't say much about the real Ed Bradley that lay beneath the icon pedestal. Fortunately, I had a chance to see that Ed Bradley. It happened in L.A. in 1998. And it didn't come from the weekly glimpse the nation got of him in front of the camera or in the stern faced, go for the jugular interviews he did with any and every one of news importance. It came off camera, and it was the simple kindness he showed to a guest and a personal expression of appreciation that he showed to me that revealed the real Ed Bradley.

Bradley and *60 Minutes* had gotten wind of a story that had tugged at the heartstrings of the nation. That was the heinous and tormenting rape and murder of a 7-year-old African-American girl Sherrice Iverson at a Nevada casino by a white teen, Jeremy Strohmeyer in May, 1997. The murder stirred even greater furor when Strohmeyer's friend, David Cash, who was at the scene, cavalierly admitted in an interview that he had knowledge of the murder but said and did nothing about it. This touched off a nationwide campaign by Sherrice's mother, Yolanda Manuel, to have Cash prosecuted as an accessory.

I had become deeply involved in the case. I assisted Ms. Manuel with the barrage of interviews, press conferences, and rallies that were held demanding the prosecution of the young man. I joined with L.A. based activist Najee Ali and other Manuel supporters in the push for tougher child protective laws. We later succeeded. In September 2000, the California state legislature passed and then Governor Gray Davis signed into law the Sherrice Iverson Good Samaritan Law which made it a crime to witness the sexual assault of a minor without notifying police.

The producers at *60 Minutes* made it clear that they regarded the story of the rape and murder as more than a story. It was a human tragedy and they wanted to make sure that that dimension came through in their piece.

The day before the scheduled interview, a *60 Minutes* producer implored me to come to the taping with Ms. Manuel. I knew that Bradley would do the interview with her, and that was enough. I knew I had to be there. I was pleasantly surprised when the producer suggested that Bradley was interested in getting a copy of my most recent book, *The Crisis in Black and Black.*

When he entered the small room that had been hastily made into a makeshift studio at the Beverly Wilshire Hotel in Beverly Hills, he smiled broadly and thanked me for the book. He thumbed through it slowly, and with that trademark pensive look, slowly and assuredly said that he looked forward to reading it. His warmth, appreciation and sincerity bowled me over. Bradley treated me as a peer and even friend.

His sincerity and warmth was on full display during and after the interview with Ms. Manuel. There was the gentle, empathetic tone in his voice when he talked to her and the soft expression on his face. It was clear he didn't consider her and the case just another news story. She was a real person to him, a mother that had suffered a traumatic loss. Bradley shared her pain.

When the interview ended he held her hand for a brief moment, and expressed his sorrow over the tragedy. He lingered for a long moment, then smiled at me, warmly shook my hand and encouraged us to stay strong. He then slowly departed. The segment as we expected was every bit the probing, in-depth, news piece we expected. More importantly, it was tinged with an uncharacteristic touch of self-righteousness, even indignation that strayed past the bounds of what's considered an objective report piece. That was vintage Ed Bradley, and we deeply appreciated that.

It was Bradley's simple gesture of kindness off camera that meant much to Ms. Manuel and me. It told us that this was a man who really cared. This was a man who was more than a top notch professional. This was a man who was a top notch human being. That's the Ed Bradley that I will always remember and revere.

*****

The applause was loud virtually every moment that Yolanda King was on stage performing her one-woman theatrical performance in May 2007. The audience showed her much love, and most importantly, appreciation for her. I sat spellbound at Agape Church in Culver City, a suburb of Los Angeles, where King performed.

The audience didn't embrace and idolize King solely because she was the daughter of Dr. Martin Luther King, Jr. Most of those in the audience weren't even born when King was alive. The applause for her wasn't solely out of a misty nostalgia for the civil rights movement. Most there had no first-hand knowledge or involvement in the civil rights battles in the 1960s. Their applause and respect was for her, and her moving recapture of the pain, suffering, and sacrifice as well as the triumphs of the civil rights movement in her performance. Their sustained applause was also given out of deep appreciation for her impassioned crusade to keep Dr. King's dream alive by actively opposing Bush's wasteful and ruinous Iraq war, championing women and gay rights, and fighting for economic justice for the poor.

In between her theatrical skits, she would pause take a deep breath, and in measured but passionate tones remind the audience that King's dream was still unfulfilled. She in turn prodded, cajoled, and implored the audience that the best way to keep her father's dream alive was to be active fighters for peace and social justice.

Yolanda King understood that decades after the great civil rights battles of the 1960s blacks were still two and three times more likely to be unemployed than whites, trapped in segregated neighborhoods, and that their kids will attend disgracefully failing, mostly segregated public schools. Despite the civil rights gains, the reality that young black males and females were far more likely to be murdered, suffer HIV/AIDS affliction, to be racially-profiled by police, imprisoned, placed on probation or parole, permanently barred in many states from voting because of felony convictions, were much more likely to receive the death penalty especially if their victims were white, and are more likely to be victims of racially motivated violence than whites.

She well knew that middle-class blacks that reaped the biggest gains from the civil rights struggles often find the new suburban neighborhoods they moved to re-segregated and soon looked like the old neighborhoods they fled. They are ignored by cab drivers, followed by clerks in stores, left fuming at restaurants because of poor or no service, find that more and more of their sons and daughters are cut out of scholarships and student support programs at universities because of the demolition of affirmative action, and denied bank loans for their businesses and homes.

Then there are the fierce battles over affirmative action, police violence, the segregation laws still on the books in some Southern states, and the still poignant memory of thousands of poor blacks fleeing for their lives from the Katrina floodwaters in New Orleans in 2005, and the big fight over what if anything should be done about the plight of the black poor. These are further bitter reminders of the gaping economic and racial chasm in America. Yolanda knew that as well, and was a resolute fighter for the poor.

In the decades after King's murder, Yolanda stormed the barricades against racial injustice, economic inequality, military adventurism, and against hate crimes and violence. She wrote countless letters, gave speeches, and participated in direct action campaigns. She continued to fiercely protect King's legacy from the opportunists that twisted and sullied his words and name.

The civil rights struggle has now become the stuff of nostalgia, history books, and the memoirs of aging former civil rights leaders. Yet, millions remain trapped in poverty, and racial discrimination still pervades much of American society. Dr. King's dream was to free them from that plight. Yolanda King and her father shared that same dream. She died in May 2007. She was 51.

Like her father she did more than dream. That came through in that her memorable moment on stage that I saw. She was more than just King's daughter.

*****

The faint smile on Mrs. Gertrude Baines face midway through my tribute remarks to her was literally a smile for the ages. I, and a small group of well-wishers, admirers, hospital staff, and reporters that gathered to pay a birthday tribute to Mrs. Baines in April, 2009 were witnesses to history; a living, breathing history filled with much pain and promise. At 115 years of age, Mrs. Baines, an African-American, had once more earned the proud and breathtaking distinction of being the world's oldest person. The *Guinness Book of Records* bestowed that title on her after a painstaking sift through stacks of official birth records. Along the way, it had discounted the claims from many others worldwide of being the world's oldest. An official from Guinness presented her with a proclamation at the birthday tribute that acknowledged her age feat.

I did not, however, give my remarks honoring Mrs. Baines to the assembled group solely because she had attained that amazing age, but rather for what she represented. At her world record shattering age and despite being permanently confined to a convalescent hospital, Mrs. Baines was still a strong role model for health and positive living. She also had a passion for the fight for justice. She was a member and solid supporter of the Main Gospel Church in Los Angeles. In November 2008, Mrs. Baines spoke proudly of how she voted for and cheered on President Obama. She considered this one of her proudest moments.

Mrs. Baines also represented something even deeper and more profound. Her father was born into slavery in 1856. She was the daughter of a slave. She was one of the few last surviving links to the horror of slavery which is still a divisive, contentious and bitter part of the African-American past. Mrs. Baines's life spanned the near century of legal Jim Crow segregation, political disfranchisement, and racial brutality that followed slavery. Her life was a tremendous living reminder of and testament to the resilience, fortitude and courage of the many African-Americans who despite the odds overcame that terrible legacy and have done so much to enrich the social tapestry of America. She died ironically on a date that is a date noted for a different reason in history. September 11, 2009. She was 115.

I was proud to be able to say that directly to Mrs. Baines at her 115th birthday celebration. I was grateful when Mrs. Baines repaid me with her smile. Mrs. Baines truly lived as the eternal Mother Spirit of a people who have come so far against so much. She was a last living link to a painful part of the African-American past.

*****

Michael Jackson as it sadly turned out was also very much a painful part of the African-American present not past. It had little to do with his secure place as the King of Pop, and his living icon status. It was the "trial." The trial was Jackson's infamous child molestation trial in 2005. Near the end of the first week of the trial, I hosted a gathering at a local cultural center in South Los Angeles that brought together a large group of African-American community activists and leaders to talk about Jackson, the trial and whether he was a target because he was a rich, successful, and famous African-American. This is the slightly paranoid tinged chatter heard whenever a black celebrity, and there have been a lot of them, wind up in the court docket for real or alleged crimes or are lambasted in the media for bad behavior.

The discussion quickly took two surprising turns. The first was an impassioned message that Jackson delivered to the group through a personal emissary. He pleaded his innocence and asked us for support. This brought a hush to the room. Then there was the second turn. The discussion shifted from talk about Jackson's trial and his sometimes on again off again, quirky, ambivalent relationship with African-Americans and his seemingly confused racial identity, to a reminder from the Jackson surrogate that Jackson wanted everyone there to know that he took great delight in his charitable work. There was no message from Jackson about his media and self-anointed title as the King of Pop, his musical icon status, the Grammys and platinum records he won, nor anything more than the perfunctory mention of his legal woes.

He clearly wanted the group to think of him as much more than an entertainer or a musician. Some present vaguely remembered that Jackson had made a splash in 1985 when he and Lionel Ritchie wrote "We Are the World" and performed the music as part of an all-star cast of singers and celebrities to raise money for African charities.

A few others vaguely remembered that Jackson forked over the $1.5 million that he got in a settlement from Pepsi in 1984 for the burn accident he suffered while filming a Pepsi commercial to the Burn Center at Brotman Hospital in Culver City. But that was it.

There were puzzled looks at the mention of Jackson's charitable giving and even more at the list of the peace and social justice related activities Jackson was involved with. At that point, most in the room listened in rapt attention at the names of the more than 40 known charities and organizations that Jackson gave to during the 1990s, both individually and through his expansively named Heal the World Foundation. The foundation was mired in a messy organizational and tax wrangle that briefly made headlines in 2002. Yet, there was virtually no press mention when Jackson jumpstarted the Foundation again in 2008 with a fresh wad of cash.

This was all new news to most of those in the room about Jackson. In fact, good news for more than a few of those who had bitterly scorned, ridiculed, and mocked him. To them Jackson was little more than a Casper-the-ghost-looking bleached skin, nose job, eye shade, straight hair and gyrating hips ambiguous black man who had made a ton of money and had been lauded, fawned over, and adored by whites. This was more than enough reason for some blacks to view him with a jaundiced eye.

For others, though, Jackson's wealth and fame didn't immunize him from being tarred by the press and many in the industry as a child molester. They felt some empathy for him and his legal battle.

In the months and years after his acquittal, debate raged over whether he was a washed up, health challenged, damaged goods, and financially strapped one time pop star who desperately wanted to snatch back a glimmer of his past glory. Or, whether he still had some of the trademark Jackson flare and talent left. Even that debate seemed to pass Jackson by since he knew that his every word and act was still instant news, and that there were still hordes of fans who would heap dreamy eyed adulation on him.

The quest to seal a legacy as more than just the Pop King told much about Jackson's desire that the small but unseen and much neglected part of his life, that is his charitable work be known and remembered. That he be remembered as more than just a black man who made his living grabbing his crotch before millions. Or a man who's other claim to notoriety was that he delighted in surrounding himself with packs of children.

The community gathering during the Jackson trial was the last time I heard in minute details the extent of Jackson's giving and the names of the organizations that he had endorsed and helped. I was glad for that moment. He died on June 25, 2009. He was 50. In the four years between the meeting in 2005 in which he appealed to us for support and his death in 2009, I had occasion to drive by his play retreat in the Santa Inez Valley. It was big, spacious, and there was a hint of mystery about it, much like its owner.

Yet, there was no mystery that Jackson had made his mark as it turned out in ways that transcended the world of pop. This is the Jackson that I want to and will always remember. This is the other Michael Jackson.

Chapter 13
On the Global Highway

Chapter 13 - On The Global Highway

I couldn't believe my luck at the invitation that came from the editors of the *Guardian* newspaper. The invitation was to join a delegation that was then euphemistically called a cultural workers group that was selected to visit the Peoples Republic of China. The group would be the first delegation of prominent American artists and writers to visit the country since Nixon had made his famed visit to China in February 1972. It was late April 1973. Candice Bergen, Burt Schneider, Howard DaSilva were some of the film notables on the delegation. They had attained prominence in film as actors, producers, and in DaSilva's case had been a black listed actor in the 1950s. Sonia Sanchez was part of the delegation. She had won numerous poetry and literary prizes. I had gained some notoriety for my op-ed columns in the *Guardian*. They had stirred discussion and even debate among many progressive activists.

My op-ed pieces on radical politics and black issues had also drawn the attention of the FBI. Twice agents were spotted in my neighborhood. One was even spotted talking to my next door neighbor about my activities. There were times that I noted a plain looking but noticeable car following me as I drove into the parking lot at KPFK radio. The driver and his passenger were always dressed in FBI Director J. Edgar Hoover's required attire for his agents of black suits, skinny ties and white shirts. They looked very straight laced.

There was a brief opening in the mid-1970s when the FBI was compelled as a result of lawsuits to release surveillance files under the

Freedom of Information Act on those deemed radical activists. I promptly applied and got my files. I read with disgust and amusement the heavily redacted lines in my file that had broad sections blacked out, presumably to protect the identities of their informants. There were notes that read as "subject was seen boarding a plane," or "subject's car was observed in the parking lot at KPFK, "or subject was a meeting of….." A friend who I showed it to quipped, "Is this what the government is wasting our tax dollars on." My retort was if this is what the FBI wants to know about me all it had to do was read one of my columns or listen to one of my broadcasts on KPFK.

The point was not that I was doing anything that could remotely be called a security threat. The spying was done partly out of Hoover's perverse obsession with salacious gossip, a faceless bureaucracy, and the FBI's well-established protocol to snoop and spy on anyone deemed radical. The FBI's spying had a life of its own that had nothing to do with the threat the subject they were spying on allegedly posed.

I was sure that my China trip would be thoroughly scrutinized by the FBI and the State Department. We were required to get permission from the State Department to make the trip. I joined the group in San Francisco and we flew on *Japan Airlines* to Tokyo where we stayed overnight, and then on to Hong Kong. It was still a self-governing British colony then, and I had a day there for sightseeing. That amounted to little more than boarding the tour bus by China Intourist service from the airport to our hotel. The tour bus departed from there early the next day. We headed North through the new territories to

Canton.

There I had my first glimpse of what many foreigners travelling to China in those days remarked on, namely the crush of persons that appeared like a moving sea of humanity on the streets. This was a sight that I'd see on every city that we visited the next two weeks. It was a whirl from there of non-stop visits to schools, communes, factories, and an opera performance. There was a visit to Mao Tse Tung's birthplace in Shaoshan and a walk through his home. In Peking (before the city was renamed Bejing), we made a day long visit and hike up the Great Wall. I spent a full day roaming through the Forbidden City.

At every stop, there was the obligatory session in which our group exchanged views with local writers and artists. I could always tell who the major Communist Party officials were by their neatly pressed Mao jackets and trousers. They wore huge buttons of Mao on their lapels. They were always polite, correct, and deeply curious about our work. In our walks through city streets, the officials would continually try to discourage gawkers from staring at us. There stares were not hostile. They were simply curious. This was the first time many of them had seen Westerners. Their efforts to shoo people away were all to no avail. We were too irresistible, a curiosity sight for them.

In Peking, our hosts reserved a special seat for us in the visitors section in Red Square for the Party's traditional annual May Day parade and salute to the revolution. There were gigantic placards with the pictures of Marx, Engels, and, of course Mao. The column of marchers paraded by the viewing stands in a seemingly never ending procession. It was colorful and breathtaking. A special moment for me came when I got a glimpse from our seats of the party leaders. With the exception of Mao whose fragile health then had become a crisis issue for the party, all the leading party leaders were there. Chou En Lai after Mao was the best known and most recognizable Chinese Communist leader. He was there. He had been by Mao's side on the Long March in the 1930s, and through the years of civil war. He was their nation's top diplomat and foreign policy expert. He was credited with facilitating with Henry Kissinger the initiative that broke the quarter century barrier between China and the U.S. and led to normalized relations. Chou sat with a stoical look in the front row of the leader's viewing section.

Despite the pomp and the relentless efforts of our hosts to show China as a big, prospering, and a rising political and economic powerhouse, China was a desperately poor country. In the countryside, conditions looked as they did in medieval times. The homes were made of straw and crude stone, farm animals were everywhere, and the villagers looked impoverished. There was also the painful sight of many older women with shrunken feet. They were the by-products of the ancient custom in pre-revolutionary China of binding young women's feet called "Lotus Feet" as a means of displaying status. As older women, they hobbled around in crippling agony.

There was also the security issue. There was one reminder that China, despite the thaw in relations with the U.S, still regarded the U.S. as a military security threat. On the plane from Shanghai to Peking, I attempted to snap a picture from the window from the air. An attendant rushed over and admonished me that pictures were forbidden in flight. Presumably, this was to guard against the possibility of taking a shot of some defense facility or military base installation. In the few hours of free time I had in Peking, I requested and got one of our hosts to take me to the Tanzanian embassy. I had pre-arranged to interview the Tanzania ambassador to China. I wanted to discuss his countries relations with China in light of the agreement made in February 1965, inked by President Julius Nyerere of Tanzania with the Chinese government. During his first visit to China then he secured agreement to assist the construction of the Tanzania-Zambia railway.

At the time it was one of the biggest aid and construction projects that China had undertaken in any foreign country. It would take three years to complete. The project was viewed as both a means to accelerate economic development, trade, and transportation between the countries, and to give China its first solid foothold in Africa. Tanzania had made a bold statement with the railroad and its close tie to China that it would not be under the thumb of the West. Nyerere was determined to chart an independent path and had embraced its version of socialism. The rail agreement lifted Tanzania to the head of the emerging nations that eschewed capitalism. It also made the nation a prime attraction to visit for black activists. This fueled my desire to know and learn more about Tanzania. The interview with the ambassador focused on the railroad, and his countries relation with China.

He talked fulsomely about the warm relations between the two countries. He also told me that his country would be hosting a major conference the following year that would bring African and Arab heads of states, diplomats and guerilla groups, then fighting against apartheid and colonial rule in Angola and Mozambique, together in a week long gathering. Tanzania, he said, was eager to have a strong participation from African-Americans. He urged me to attend. I filed this away.

At every hotel we stayed at, anything of value be it paper, batteries, toilet items, and combs that we routinely threw half used in the trash, on our return had disappeared from the trash. Our discards were their treasures. They were true practitioners of waste not, want not. The final evening we had a grand banquet with piles of traditional Chinese delicacies; roasted Peking Duck, wontons, roast pork, fish, dumplings and tofu. There were multiple toasts to friendship and the plum wine flowed freely. We eagerly guzzled the liquor down.

Then there was the exchange of gifts. I was given an abridged volume of the collected poems of Mao. In return, I gave my designated recipient a pen set. The next day we walked through a small gauntlet of our interpreters and local party officials, and the travel committee sponsors who were there to bid us good bye as we boarded our bus to the airport. It was a moving moment when I felt a genuine, sincere friendship and the desire for peace and goodwill between our two nations.

Only two years earlier, China and the U.S. had been implacable foes. It appeared then the two nation's clashing systems, capitalism and communism, were so incompatible that détente was unattainable. That didn't prove to be the case. Regardless, our tour was strictly a people to people tour. I felt richly rewarded and fulfilled for the experience. I would have stories to tell for months even years about being one of the first to see and experience first-hand a country which had been closed and forbidden to Americans for so many decades.

The death of Mao in September, 1976, and Deng Xiaoping's shift of the nation to a market economy transformed China especially the big cities from streets that I saw filled with bikes, rickshaws and carts to streets choked with cars, factories and pollution, big shiny new skyscrapers, chic boutiques, restaurants, and expressways. The China of the 21st Century contained no visible trace of the people on the streets dressed in the regimented drab style uniform that was prevalent during my visit. They had long since been replaced by the latest in smartly tailored Western fashions. The young were not listening to martial music but hip hop and rap.

Despite the party leaders' constant official declaration that China was still officially a Communist country ruled by the Communist Party, the China I visited was a China that no longer existed. However, it would remain forever in my memory.

*****

The China trip fueled my urge and need to see how life was in countries that purported to be radical in their political philosophy and were in conflict with the U.S. In the U.S. the standard line was that the socialist and especially Communist countries were oppressive, regimented, and their people were poor, downtrodden and victimized. The U.S., by contrast, was the world's beacon of freedom. I wanted to believe that this was just drum beat Cold War propaganda that flowed from the fact that the U.S. and the West were locked in an intense and prolonged battle to prevent the spread of socialism among the newly emerging nations in Africa and Asia. This thought was in my mind when I received another invitation in September 1976 to be part of another delegation of progressive writers and I readily accepted. The destination this time was the Soviet Union. The official invitation came from the Young Communist League's Komsomol organization.

This time there were no hitches on the flight. It was a direct flight from New York's Kennedy Airport to Moscow on the Soviet government's official airlines, *Aerofloat*. The in-flight attendants were solicitous and fell over themselves providing us with unlimited drinks, and in flight choice food items. I wasn't sure if this was because of our quasi-official status as a delegation under the auspices of an official Soviet organization or not. I wasn't about to question the service received that befit royalty.

On arrival, we were met by three busses from the official Soviet Intourist agency and to the historic Hotel Moskva where we stayed. The next few days were filled with tours of factories, institutes, meetings with government officials and receptions. I soon had a desperate urge to break away from the routine and explore the back streets and allies of Moscow. I wanted to get a real feel of what life was really like on the streets away from the always constant presence of the official hosts. This would be my gauge to determine just how free or restricted Soviet citizens were. The two days I had to explore, I stood in line with other spectators at the Lenin Mausoleum in Red Square to view Lenin's body. I noted that this waxy figure that was perfectly preserved, was short, and had pronounced oriental features. The founder of Bolshevism, the father of the Russian Revolution and the first communist state, even in death a half century later was still the eternal bogeyman to the capitalist West.

I shopped at the giant GUM department store facing Red Square. It was cavernous, and filled with all types of goods and clothing apparel. I was conscious that I stuck out and was a foreigner. The shoppers seemed instinctively to know I was an American. I was constantly approached with offers to sell me every sort of black market item; rings, watches, liquor, clothing items. They desperately wanted to get American dollars which were worth their weight in gold on the currency exchange market in Russia.

At night I stopped at a restaurant that was billed as authentic Uzbekistani. I wanted to sample the vaunted central Asian cuisine. When I entered I was immediately greeted by three diners. Two of whom were from Uzbekistan. The other identified himself as a professor at Moscow University. They did not speak a word of English, and I did not speak a word of Russian. Still, for more than two hours we talked, in our respective languages. We managed to completely understand each other. This proved that language barriers did not have to get in the way of good personal feelings, and a genuine desire to share our experiences from two radically different cultures, worlds, and systems. In that moment we were just diners enjoying a sumptuous meal of Central Asian delicacies, complete with the mandatory shots of vodka and caviar. There were many toasts and promises to stay in touch.

On the way back to the hotel, I again crossed Red Square. I was approached by two women who seemingly came out of nowhere. They looked around in furtive and nervous glances and in broken English told me that they were Baptists and that they wanted to receive Bibles from America. They pleaded with me to help them. I politely told them that I was a guest of the Soviet government and could not help them. I hastened away. Smuggling was a serious offense, and I did not know whether this was a legitimate, though ill-gotten, request, or something else. In any case, I walked quickly away and didn't look back. The Soviet Union was officially an atheist state. And even though then there was a somewhat more relaxed attitude toward religion, it still had no official support. It was seen as rather a harmless vice, and tolerated. It was no real threat to communist institutional power. I was a visitor, an American visitor, and the last thing I needed was to get embroiled with Soviets that were in defiance of a state dictum.

Two days later we took an overnight express to Minsk in Byelorussia (today Belarus). We embarked on the usual tour of factories, and schools. The most significant meeting though was with Soviet veterans of World War II. These aging soldiers had fought in the great bloody battles of the War. They were bedecked with a sea of medals. One of them was introduced as a Hero of the Soviet Union. He talked expansively about his combat role. At times his eyes glazed over as if he were reliving the horrific moments in the trenches, and the joy and exhilaration of beating back the fascists in a war that he and the official parlance always referred to as the great patriotic war.

From Minsk, we boarded an overnight sleeper train to Leningrad. There were more meetings. The high point here was the day spent at the Winter Palace and Hermitage. This was the jewel in the crown, the holy shrine, the monument to the triumph of the Bolshevik revolution. The façade of the storming of the Winter Palace was immortalized in Sergei Eisenstein's 1927 film. The palace had been the three hundred year home to the Romanov's rule and power in pre-revolutionary czarist Russia.

Its world renowned art treasures and jewels were on full display. Our tour guides took great pains to point out that these treasures were genuine people's treasures that were bought and paid for with the toil and sweat of the Russian peasants and workers. Our final day, September 9, 1976, Moscow TV stations were filled with news of the death of Mao. I was desperate to know how Soviet commentators were spinning Mao's death. This was state run TV and everything said was the official Soviet party line. This is what stirred my curiosity because of the long, bitter conflict between China and the Soviet Union over their widely differing respective paths and views of socialism and world revolution.

Mao had forcefully opposed the Soviets in their view of socialism. I asked my host to translate what was being said. He was extremely reluctant and every question I asked was met with an indifferent shrug and vague answers. I was certain from my China trip four years earlier, that the death of Mao, so deified in China, would launch a period of deep mourning there. What I didn't realize then was that it would also usher in a period of profound change and shift in the country's economic and more subtly, its political direction. I also sensed that even though from outwards appearance in the Soviet Union, it was still firmly a Communist state, there were rumblings of change coming there too; change which in time would result in its disappearance.

Our hosts were ever gracious, wishing us good luck as we made our way to our tour busses and headed for the airport. One gave me a picture of himself and his friends and swore that one day he would come to America and look me up. He promised to write regularly. I knew the likelihood of that was slim, given the wide gulf between our two countries, and the still very formidable Cold War cleavage between the U.S. and the Soviet Union. Still, it was a nice touch; a humane gesture of friendship, that I deeply appreciated. It showed once again that warring, hostile systems are one thing, but people are people, the same everywhere. Human warmth and commonality can always trump ideology. I saw the human face in the Soviet Union, and that was the best hope for that country's future.

Chapter 14
A Third World Journey

Chapter 14 - A Third World Journey

The people to people delegations to communist countries such as China were the type of foreign travel that was popular then in activist journalist circles. A couple of months after I returned from China I remembered the Tanzanian ambassador's admonition to me in Peking to attend the 6th Pan African Congress gathering in Dar es Salaam, Tanzania in June 1974. I immediately contacted the American organizers of the trip and wrangled an invitation to be part of the African-American student delegation to the gathering.

The African trip would be memorable. I would have the experience of recording the proceedings, interviewing and rubbing shoulders with African heads of states, diplomats, government leaders, and the leaders of SWAPO, ANC, ZANU, ZAPO, and FRELIMO. These groups were fighting prolonged battles against the apartheid regime in South Africa, and the Portuguese colonial rulers in Mozambique and Angola. The trip, though, started out with an almost comical series of mishaps. The charter flight that I was told would be waiting when I got to Kennedy Airport in New York for the first leg of the trip to London had been cancelled. That set off a scramble to find another flight. Yvonne, I and other stranded delegation members sat in the waiting room for a full day and well into the evening before a flight was arranged. In London, the connecting flight to Dar es Salaam was delayed for a day. That meant a forced stay at a hotel for the night. Then we woke to find that the time for the departing flight had been changed to an earlier hour. We made it to London's Heathrow Airport just as the last passengers were boarding.

Meanwhile, the number of delegates had grown exponentially. A parade of would be delegates sporting dashikis, kofi caps, carrying conga drums, canes and walking sticks, and sporting Malcom X tee shirts, poured onto the plane. They were pumped up. They kept up a constant din of shouts and chatter during the flight. At the stop in Nairobi, Kenya, Queen Mother Moore, 75 then, who was considered the matriarch of the Black Nationalist movement, rushed out the door and skipped down the steps. She shouted "I'm home, and then fell to ground on the tarmac of the runway and kissed it. I was later told that she had done this on previous trips to the continent. Each time she milked the drama for all it was worth. Finally after the marathon of mishaps, we landed in Dar es Salaam. We were haphazardly assembled in various groups to board a line of charter busses that were waiting. The trip from the airport into the city was the first shock for many of the very middle class, black students and professors, who were dressed in their perfectly coifed designer dashikis. The groaning poverty of a Third World country hit them with blunt force. There were packs of beggars, and panhandlers in soiled, tattered clothes, the women walked the roads with baskets on their heads, and the farmers had their goats in tow. We passed rows of thatched huts, and shanty towns with open sewers. They were filled with garbage and refuse. The bus bounced, shook and rattled as it sped down the narrow, rutted road. It passed busses with passengers hanging helter skelter off the top and the sides of the busses.

One young woman repeatedly mumbled "I didn't know it was like this." The story book notion of an Africa of emperors, kings, and queens in gold and jeweled robes, sitting on diamond studded thrones and reigning over princely domains flew out the window fast. Tanzania had gotten its independence from British colonial rule barely a decade earlier in 1962. The brutal reality was that Tanzania, the host country for the Conference, was then even by African standards at the bottom of the world's poverty barrel in per capita income. Its economy was primarily rural, and agrarian. Many parts of the country seemed unchanged from what it looked like in the 19th century.

The second shock came when we were shuttled off the bus at the University of Dar es Salaam on the outskirts of the city. We were put up in dorm rooms that were slightly larger than a monk's chambers, with common bathing facilities, and no hot water. By then, Yvonne and I, had resigned ourselves to the obvious fact this wasn't America, and the comforts that we took for granted; hot water, steady electricity, supermarkets, were nowhere to be found.

The lack of comforts was soon forgotten in our rush of excitement over the conference. I attended many of the main sessions. I listened to President Nyerere give an impassioned welcoming address and Guinean President Sekou Toure give a keynote address. The poet Amiri Baraka presented a paper on culture and Pan-Africanism at one of the conference symposiums He later held forth on the subject to our group at the dining room table at the university. In between, numerous speakers filled the hall with denunciations of racial and colonial rule, and vowed to fight to the death until they had overthrown the white regimes. In the next decade, many of the heads of the established guerrilla groups that I heard speak would become the heads of state. One of the most notable was Robert Mugabe, who then headed the Zimbabwe African Nation Union, ZANU. In 2015 he was still the President of Zimbabwe. He was roundly pilloried by Western leaders for his alleged despotism, and strong arm rule. This made him a pariah to the West.

Many of the leaders of the guerilla movements held forth at the numerous receptions that were given at various sites around the city. I chatted briefly with the Vice President of Tanzania. He assured me that the country had an ambitious program of development, trade, and agriculture, and that in time Tanzania and other African nations would make big strides toward catching up with the West in development. Near the end of the conference, I joined with several delegates and hopped on a motor launch going over to Zanzibar. The fabled island of spice had been incorporated at independence into what was then Tanganyika, the colonial name of the country. The stay here offered another surprise. The hotel we stayed at was unlike any hotel in the capital. It was a virtual palace, with ornate columns, and a distinct Arab architectural style. The government had invested heavily in making Zanzibar tourist friendly. The hotel it built would rate anywhere as a five star hotel with top grade food and accommodations. The aim was to draw more Europeans to the country and their dollars.

In the 18th and 19th Centuries, Zanzibar had been a major embarkation for Arab slavers trafficking in the thousands of Africans from the interior to the Arab peninsula, where they served as slaves, body guards, eunuchs, and domestics for the Arab sheiks, kings and princes. A guest host at the hotel drove us in the afternoon to the Mangapwani Slave Chamber which was a square underground cell that was cut out of coralline rock with a roof on top where the slaves were held before being loaded onto the dhows and transported across the Red Sea to their plight.

My wife and my friend from my days at Cornell, Dwight Bachman and his wife Portia, hammed it up and took turns snapping shots with their hands in the iron rings that held the chains where the slaves were shackled. The hotel staff hosted a party for us later that day on the beach. The white sands and deep blue of the Indian Ocean shimmered in the tropical sun.

This was the closest I thought you could come to Paradise. It contrasted sharply with conditions on the mainland. I departed with a small group the day before the final session of the conference. I did not want a repeat of the travel ordeal I had suffered through getting to the conference. As the plane lifted off, I felt joy and sadness; joy that I had fulfilled a dream of visiting the African continent which I and other black activists had transformed in our imagination into the mecca of black pride and glory. I was sad though at the realization that Africa was still very much a work in progress and that it would take decades to recover from the centuries of devastation, of slavery, pillage, colonial rape and rule. Still, I had seen Africa, and for the moment that was satisfying enough.

I had visited the Soviet Union and China when they were avowedly communist, and Tanzania when it was avowedly embarking on its version of socialism. I wanted to complete my tours of avowedly countries that adhered to Marxist ideology to see how life was there. This left only one remaining country that fit my need: Cuba. I had long bemoaned the fact that in 1969, I had an opportunity to visit the island as part of a small delegation of African-American writers, scholars, and activists. However, that was one of those occasions when I let the fear and doubt of family members about me traveling there influence me.

They were concerned about the danger to my personal safety in travelling to Cuba. It was then constantly in the news as a haven for Black Panthers and other radical activists fleeing from the law in the U.S. There had been airplane hijackings to Cuba, and the country had offered some of the hijackers asylum. This was on top of the long running effort by the U.S. through a relentless campaign of subversion, invasion, and assassination attempts to get rid of Castro. The time did seem fraught with peril. I declined to go and later heard from some of the members of the group that they had waited for me an entire day in Mexico City to arrive before departing. In those days, one had to either fly to Havana from Mexico or Canada. I felt even worse when I heard this. So Cuba still had a call on me to visit.

The chance finally came in June 2004, when my daughter, Sikivu, a writer, got an invitation to attend a writer's conference in Havana. I had my opening. When I suggested to her that I'd like to tag along, she was ecstatic. We would travel together. This would be one of several international trips we had taken together over the years to a Latin or Caribbean country together; the Bahamas, and Mexico three times. Cuba would blend both. The timing was right for our trip. President George W. Bush had opened a small opening by authorizing a direct flight from Miami to Havana on American Airlines for humanitarian purposes to allow Cuban families to visit relatives. It had proven popular. This was a mild thaw in the low intensity war between the two countries. As a journalist, and a writer, my daughter and I sought and got the official approval to make the trip.

The one reminder at Miami International airport about the still frozen relations between the Cuba and the U.S. came at the airport. We were required to check in an extra hour before departure for security purposes we were told. We had to run a gauntlet of screeners, baggage checkers, document checkers, body searches, and metal detectors. This was just to get on the plane. The overwhelming majority of the passengers were Cuban. I surmised that they were taking advantage of the chance to visit family members.

I had my nose pressed to the window the entire short flight of 90 miles to Havana. As we neared the island I stared continually at its land shape and the greenery of the country. Jose Marti airport had the feel of a mid-sized Mid-Western airport. As we went into the terminal, there were loud shouts and cheers from a thick mass of waiting relatives and friends of the arriving American Cuban passengers. There were smiles, shouts of joy and tearful embraces. It was truly a great coming home for many of them.

Along the road, in the taxi ride to our downtown hotel there were the giant pictures of Che Guevara and Fidel Castro with revolutionary slogans. Other than that there was almost a total absence of any commercial billboards and advertisements that are ubiquitous in other Caribbean countries for any and every product. This was the Cuba, revolutionary Cuba, and the absence of a Western commercial imprint seemed to me emblematic of revolution and its defiance of the US since Castro seized power in 1959 and rode triumphantly into Havana. That completed a revolution that had been in the making for years. The revolution held such promise for poor and working class Cubans. At the same time, it ignited an unprecedented flight from the island of middle class, and wealthy Cuban businessmen, bankers, professionals and academics to the U.S.

Their flight and the effect of the half century of a crippling trade embargo clamped on the island were very much evident on the streets. The city appeared as if time had stood still in 1959. The buildings in downtown Havana were deteriorated, cracked, with paint peeling. There were the vintage 1950s Fords, Chevys, Buicks, and Cadillac's on the streets which were polished and shined and kept running with cobbled together parts, and replacements. There were also many Toyotas, Hondas, and small foreign models on the streets too.

We made the rounds of the plazas, the revolutionary museum, Revolution Square, and took a taxi up to the home of Ernest Hemingway up in the hills outside above Havana. Hemingway had popularized Cuba for American writers as a haunt in pre Castro Cuba. We generously sampled the Cuban cuisine at several upscale restaurants that catered to foreigners, primarily Europeans and Canadians.

The one area of Cuban life that I was especially interested in was race relations. Cuban officials had long touted the revolution had ended the vicious racism that had marked Cuban history from slavery to their revolution. Cuba's whites were at the top of the pecking order in all areas of economic and political life before 1959. But there was steady criticism in articles by Afro-Cubans, such as Cuban expatriate Carlos Moore in *Cuba—The Untold Story*, that hotly disputed that contention. Without question, the blacks in Cuba at the lower end had benefited from free health care, education and the island's social net.

So what was the truth? I noted that with the exception of one tour guide who was dark-skinned, all the others who regularly interacted with foreigners at the swank hotels and restaurants were white or fair skinned. At the *Havana Libre* hotel all the clerks, reservation, concierge and waiters were white or fair skinned. It was subtle but at these businesses that catered primarily to Europeans this seemed a nod to their presumed racial tastes. In any case, racism had never been as virulent and officially institutionalized by law as in the U.S. It was still a part of Cuban life, though. It was an issue increasingly of troubling concern to black Cubans, and hopefully the Cuban government.

*****

The flight back from Marti airport was again packed with Cuban –

American visitors returning from family visits to the island. As the plane, touched down at Miami International Airport, the Cubans cheered and shouted, and a few tried to do an impromptu dance in their seats. Their ties were still firmly with Cuba but America was there home. I took their joy at arriving back as less a knock at Cuba that was still under an embargo and still was an impoverished country, then the hard reality that America was a big, wealthy nation that had far more opportunities than Cuba. Still, they had gone and that in itself was a positive affirmation that Cuba had survived the worst, and was still intact.

A decade after my Cuba visit, I took two big takeaways from President Obama's Cuban opening in December 2014. The first was obvious. After 55 years of U.S.-backed invasions, covert efforts to sabotage and overthrow Fidel Castro, an embargo, and a Cold War freeze in diplomatic relations, the U.S. policy toward Cuba has been an abject failure. Raul Castro remains the official government head, and Fidel, is still a presence in Cuban life and a bigger than ever figure internationally. Obama took the logical step that almost certainly would have been taken years ago, except for a politically retrograde GOP and older, politically connected Cuban Americans, and that is to normalize relations with the island.

Obama pointed to the obvious when he said the old policies, meaning containment and subversion, didn't "make sense." More Cubans are travelling to wherever they can get a visa, political dissent and expression is more open than ever, and there are more private owned businesses and farms in Cuba. While Cuba is still officially a one party-state, Cuban leaders have repeatedly made clear they are committed to real reforms. In an extended visit to Cuba a decade ago, I saw firsthand the changes in tourism, trade, and people-friendly relations in Havana and other cities that I visited.

I left Cuba, satisfied, that I had done something in my lifetime that few Americans had done. That was travel to four countries, Cuba when it was officially communist, Russia when it was the Soviet Union, China when it was the Peoples Republic of China, and Tanzania when it embraced Pan Africanism and Socialism. This was my grand political travel slam. I saw and compared two hostile, distinctly opposite systems, capitalism and communism, and saw up close how the socialist and communist systems had affected the lives of its people. This was their past that I had seen. I had lived to see the monumental change in that system that marked their present and future.

Chapter 15
From King
to Obama

Chapter 15 - From King to Obama

I detected a note of anxiety in her voice in the voice mail she left me urging me to call her as soon as possible. It was late summer, 2014. She was a key White House staffer. I had spoken to her on several occasions in the past and she always had a relaxed, but business like tone when we talked about a particular policy initiative from President Obama that she wanted to insure I knew about and perhaps would discuss on my weekly KPFK radio talk show. This time was different. I immediately called her back. She made it clear that our conversation was strictly off the record. I agreed.

She was concerned that GOP Congressional leaders might well follow through on their threat to introduce an impeachment measure against Obama in Congress.

This was not a false fear. Various GOP congresspersons, conservative commentators, bloggers, and talk show hosts had been screaming for Obama's head. The charge against him was that he had made a mighty effort to impose an "imperial presidency" on the nation by abusing his power to issue executive orders and refusing to work with Congress on key issues. This charge was almost always accompanied by tossing out the words "arrogant," "indifferent," and "callous" to describe his alleged nose thumb at Congress.

None of this was true. It was yet another cynical and calculated move to malign, weaken, and render ineffectual Obama's presidency. The White House staffer, though, said that the move might not happen but the White House wanted to be prepared to act if it developed any real legs. As someone who had a voice and a constituency in the media, I and other White House friends could be helpful in mobilizing instant support to beat back the impeachment talk.

The fear she expressed to me of a full blown frontal assault on Obama cast yet another frightening glare on the relentless, and savage, efforts of the GOP from the moment that Obama stepped into the White House in January, 2009 to undermine his presidency. The ostensible reason was the ferocious and never ending ideological and partisan warfare that waged between Democrats and Republicans for three decades since the Reagan years in the 1980s. The real reason I and many others suspected was race.

This was the bittersweet consequence of making history as the first African-American president in the nation's history. In a real sense, Obama was the culmination of the six decade fight to end the political enslavement of blacks. The South had a storehouse of tactics to accomplish that; poll taxes, literacy tests, naked intimidation, and violence. The fight against political disenfranchisement began in the 1940s and 1950s, and gathered major steam in the 1960s culminating in the passage of the 1965 Voting Rights Act. In the near half century after the passage of act and on the eve of Obama's White House entrance in 2009, a political revolution had occurred. There were thousands of blacks holding governorships, senate and congressional, state and local offices in the South and nationally.

The fight to make that political revolution was waged by nameless thousands in dozens of marches, rallies, demonstrations, in many backwater locales throughout the South. This often had horrific and violent bloody endings in places such as Selma, Alabama in March 1965.

However, the undisputed titular, symbolic, and real driving force for the political revolution was Dr. King. It could be truthfully said that King was the reason for Obama.

It was more than fitting when his inauguration in 2009 fell on the national day of celebration for King. It was even more fitting that he took the oath of office on the bible that King used.

More than any other resident of the White House, Obama understood that King is a big reason for his political success. Then Democratic presidential candidate Obama first publicly expressed deep gratitude to King and the civil rights movement in a speech in Selma, Alabama in March, 2007. This was just the start of Obama's firmly drawing the line between King and himself.

*****

I knew even before the announcement was made that the Democrats would embrace King's legacy at the Democratic National Convention in Denver in August, 2008. Obama would formally accept the party's nomination as its presidential candidate. The convention coincided with the 45th anniversary of the Historic March on Washington. The march was the gold standard in defining the next generation of social and political activism in America. Obama was the new gold standard for measuring the progress and gains that America had made since then.

The final day of the Democratic National Convention, Obama would speak and accept the nomination. I listened as Obama in rising tones said, "They could've heard words of anger and discord. They could've been told to succumb to the fear and frustration of so many dreams deferred."

"But what the people heard instead ... is that in America our destiny is inextricably linked,"

Today, "America, we cannot turn back.... We must pledge once more to march into the future." John Lewis, the last living major participant of the Selma march reinforced the connection when he told the crowd that King's dream is still alive.

The Democrats made doubly sure that the King-Obama connection wasn't missed. It gave Bernice King and Martin Luther King III prominent spots on the speaker's bill immediately before Obama spoke. Both of King's children directly referenced King's famed words describing his dream of racial justice for America.

King III said his father would be proud of both Obama and "the America that will elect him."

Even if Democratic presidential contender Obama hadn't uttered King's name once in his Democratic presidential acceptance speech, the legacy of King and the civil rights movement would still have hung heavy over Denver's Invesco Field. Obama's meticulously scripted decision to break convention tradition and give his acceptance speech in an open air site on the 45th anniversary of the March on Washington dispelled the myth that Obama was a post-civil rights generation African-American politician.

To his credit Obama never bought into the myth. It would be hard for him to anyway. He frequently praised King and the civil rights movement, and said he has read and studied closely King's writings and speeches. Even if he hadn't read a word of King's speeches, Obama was not just the symbolic embodiment of the civil rights struggle. He was an embodiment of the still unfinished business of the civil rights movement. That's with one added caveat and a risk. The caveat is that the civil rights challenges that King faced and that he so eloquently spoke of in his "I Have a Dream" speech a half century ago are even more complex a half century after the March on Washington. The risk was the great temptation to see Obama's historic candidacy as the end not the continuation of the civil rights battles.

The checklist of problems that King faced and Obama has faced includes astronomically high unemployment among young blacks, gaping racial disparities in the criminal justice system, re-segregation of neighborhoods and schools, rampant housing discrimination, racial glass ceilings in corporate hiring and promotions, black family instability among the black poor, police abuse, racial profiling, and racially motivated hate crimes.

There are challenges that King didn't have to deal, or were barely issues a half century ago. One of those is that race problems in America are no longer exclusively a black and white problem. That's because blacks are no longer America's top minority. Latinos are. Immigration reform, the English Only wars, and the fight for political empowerment are the new civil rights concerns.

Obama also faced a glaring problem that King had only begun to wrestle with in his last days. That's the plight of the urban black poor. As America unraveled in the 1960s in the anarchy of urban riots, campus takeovers, and anti-war street battles, the civil rights movement and its leaders fell apart, too. Many of them fell victim to their own success and failure. When they broke down the racially restricted doors of corporations, government agencies, and universities, middle class blacks, not the poor, rushed headlong through them. More than four decades later there are now two black Americas. The fat, rich, and comfortable black America of Oprah Winfrey, Robert Johnson, Bill Cosby, Condoleezza Rice, Denzel Washington and the legions of millionaire black athletes and entertainers, businesspersons and professionals. They have grabbed a big slice of America's pie.

*****

The black America of the poor is fragmented and politically rudderless. Lacking competitive technical skills and professional training, and shunned by many middle-class black leaders, they have been shoved even further to the outer margins of American society. The chronic problems of gang, and drug violence, family breakdown, police abuse, the soaring incarceration rate of young black males, the mounting devastation of HIV and AIDS disease in black communities, abysmally failing inner city public schools have made things even worse for them.

Then there's the political rise of, and influence of black conservatives, the black evangelicals, and the rancorous internal fights among blacks over gay marriage, gay rights, and abortion have tormented, perplexed, and forced civil rights leaders, who are mostly liberal Democrats to confront their own gender and political biases. They have tried to strike a halting, tenuous balance between their liberalism and the social conservatism of many blacks.

Obama's decision to peg his acceptance speech to the March on Washington was not mere showy campaign symbolism. It stood as a fitting tribute to the civil rights movement that challenged the nation to make King's dream of justice and equality a reality. Obama faced that challenge as a community organizer, civil rights attorney, during his stints in the Illinois legislature and in the Senate. He'd face that same challenge in the White House. And that could hardly be called post-civil rights.

Five years after Obama firmly tied his presidency and the history of the struggle that made it possible for him to attain that presidency to King, the opportunity rose again to link the two.

That was the fiftieth anniversary of the March on Washington. It was accompanied by a wave of commemorative events that tried hard to recapture the energy and the spirit of the 1963 March. This was a tall order. The original march punctuated by King's memorable "I Have a

Dream" speech acted as a powerful wrecking ball that crumbled the walls of legal segregation and ushered in an era of unbridled opportunities for many blacks. The results are unmistakable today. Blacks are better educated, more prosperous, own more businesses, hold more positions in the professions, have more elected officials, and high-ranking corporate officials, managers, and executives than ever before.

Yet the many racial improvements that the 1963 March on Washington symbolized, mask the harsh reality that the times and challenges fifty years later were far different and in some ways far more daunting than what King and the civil rights leaders that organized the famed march faced.

When King marched in 1963 black leaders had already firmly staked out the moral high ground for a powerful and irresistible civil rights movement. It was classic good versus evil. Many white Americans were sickened by the gory news scenes of baton-battering racist Southern sheriffs, fire hoses, police dogs, and Klan violence unleashed against peaceful black protesters. Racial segregation was considered by just about anyone and everyone who fancied themselves as decent Americans as immoral and indefensible, and the civil rights leaders were hailed as martyrs and heroes in the fight for justice.

As America unraveled in the 1960s in the anarchy of urban riots, campus takeovers, and anti-war street battles, the civil rights movement and its leaders fell apart, too. Many of them fell victim to their own success and failure. When they broke down the racially restricted doors of corporations, government agencies, and universities, middle class blacks, not the poor, were the ones who rushed headlong through them. As King veered toward left radicalism and embraced the rhetoric of the militant anti-war movement, he became a political pariah shunned by the White House, as well as mainstream white and black leaders.

King's murder in 1968 was the turning point for race relations in America. The self-destruction from within and political sabotage from outside of black organizations left the black poor organizationally fragmented and politically rudderless. The black poor lacking competitive technical skills and professional training, and shunned by many middle-class black leaders, became expendable jail and street and cemetery fodder. Some turned to gangs, guns, and drugs to survive.

A Pew Study specifically released to coincide with the 50th anniversary celebrations graphically made the well-documented point that the economic and social gaps between whites and African-Americans have widened over the last few decades despite massive spending by federal and state governments, every imaginable state and federal civil rights law on the books, and two decades of affirmative action programs. The racial polarization that has been endemic between blacks and whites on everything from the George Zimmerman trial to just about every other controversial case that involves black and white perceptions of the workings of the criminal justice system.

A half-century later the task of redeeming King's dream meant confronting the crisis problems of family breakdown, the rash of shamefully failing public schools, racial profiling, urban police violence, the obscene racial disparities in the prison and criminal justice system, and the HIV/AIDS crisis. These are beguiling problems that sledgehammer the black poor and these are the problems that King and the civil rights movement of his day only had begun to recognize and address. Civil rights leaders today also had to confront something else that King did not have to confront. King had the sympathy and goodwill of millions of whites, politicians, and business leaders in the peak years of the civil rights movement. Much of that goodwill has vanished in the belief that blacks have attained full equality.

I was mindful that the few times Obama gave his mild, cautious thoughts about a controversial racial issue. The Trayvon Martin slaying by George Zimmerman in 2013 was a prime example. He spoke out on it and he caught much flack for it.

*****

Then there's the reality that race matters in America can no longer be framed exclusively in black and white. Latinos and Asians have become major players in the fight for political and economic empowerment and figure big in the political strategies of Democratic and Republican presidential contenders. Civil rights leaders would have to figure out ways to balance the competing and contradictory needs of these and other ethnic groups and patch them into a workable coalition for change.

It was grossly unfair to expect civil rights leaders a half century after

King to be the charismatic, aggressive champions of, and martyrs for, civil rights that he was. Or to think that fifty years later another March on Washington could solve the seemingly intractable problems of the black poor. The times and circumstances have changed too much for that. Still civil rights leaders could draw strength from King's courage, vision and dedication and fight the hardest they could against racial and economic injustices that have hardly disappeared. This was still a big and significant step toward again redeeming King's dream.

It's no accident that the trajectory from King to Obama and the civil rights battles that form that trajectory was a catalyst for and a parallel to the gay, women's, immigrant rights, farmworkers, environmental, peace movements. It had a major effect on the music, literature, and film. Many of the artists during that half century have paid homage to the civil right movement in various ways in their works.

White House Senior Advisor and Special Assistant to Obama, Valerie Jarrett and I talked at length in several on air conversations in 2011 on my radio show and afterwards about the influence of the civil rights movement on White House actions from jobs to education to health care battles Obama has waged with the GOP. She was emphatic in one of our conversations that Obama was able to galvanize support from wide segments of the American public for his initiatives in these areas. Despite the harsh attacks on him she assured me that he was optimistic about the future of the country.

It was that optimism that propelled the changes in America from the late 1950s on. It was that same optimism that inspired and influenced many of those figures we now regard as pioneers and pathfinders in politics and the arts. Their saga underlay the half century from King to Obama. This is the saga that I witnessed.

Postscript - Witness to a Turbulent History

My father was fully energized by the fast developing events in the South in 1964. In particular, he followed closely the actions of Dr. King and the Southern Christian Leadership Conference. Whenever, a civil rights leader fresh from the battles in the South came to Los Angeles to speak, usually at a local black church, he would attend. Invariably I'd go with him. On Sunday, February 21, 1965, SCLC's gruff, blunt speaking, Reverend Fred Shuttlesworth, who co-founded SCLC with Dr. King, was the featured speaker at an SCLC sponsored event at L.A.'s Second Baptist Church. My father and I sat close to the front. Shuttlesworth had barely begun to speak, when an aide, quickly walked to his side and slipped a note to him. Shuttlesworth took a long glance at it. Then without missing a beat, he bluntly said, "Malcolm X has been shot in New York. He's dead." Then without missing another beat he said "Those who live by the sword die by it."

There was a hush in the church. Shuttlesworth's words were intemperate, insensitive, and inappropriate about Malcolm's murder. Mainstream civil rights organizations regarded Malcolm as a violence prone, black extremist. He was a thorn to them. So Shuttlesworth simply reflected that view in his off the cuff remark about Malcolm. When the realization finally sank in of Malcolm's murder, there were sad looks on more than a few in the audience. I was unsettled by the news. I knew little about Malcolm at the time. Yet, I felt something terrible, even sinister had happened. I was a witness on the day to a tragic and turbulent occurrence in history.

I was reminded of Shuttlesworth's biting words about Malcolm X's assassination and then remembered how I felt often over the years after he said them. It reinforced my conviction that any compelling eyewitness memoir must never be a dry recitation of events, places and things. It must inhale life into a remembrance of those individuals whose lives not only enriched the pageant of history but did much to shape it. *From King to Obama: Witness to a Turbulent History*, as the title implies, strived to be such a work.

The individuals I spotlighted in this remembrance made contributions that are deep, rich and abiding in music, film, sports, and politics. They were scholars, political leaders, civil rights and radical movement leaders, writers, actors, musicians, and entertainers. They all were pioneers, pathfinders, and genuine cultural, political and social change agents.

They are revered today for the accomplishments and contributions they made to their respective fields and to American and international events. The period that I chronicled was, and is, one of the most profound periods in American history. It was a period of tremendous turmoil, upheaval and change. In *From King to Obama: Witness to a Turbulent History*, I sought to take the reader on a journey of discovery, my journey, back to a look at the personalities and events that marked this era in American history. The reader met them in the same way that I saw them, talked with them, and engaged them.

This book was as much an attempt to give my impressions of and my personal interaction with the leading luminaries of the era as to memorialize their memory not as legends and icons, but as real persons. Above all, *From King to Obama: Witness to a Turbulent History* was my personal tribute to those who made magnificent contributions and refreshing breakthroughs in politics, the arts, music, film, and sports. They remain the stuff of legend today. I was proud to be a witness to their accomplishments and to be able to tell that story.

About the Author

Earl Ofari Hutchinson is a nationally acclaimed author and social issues commentator. He is a syndicated columnist and a feature contributor to the Huffington Post. His columns have appeared in the *Christian Science Monitor, Chicago Tribune, Washington Post, the San Francisco Chronicle, the Los Angeles Times, Newsday, and the Baltimore Sun.*

Hutchinson is the author of ten books on race and social change in America.

He is the National Political Writer for New America Media and the *Los Angeles Wave Newspaper.* He hosts two syndicated public affairs and issues radio talk shows on KTYM Radio and KPFK Pacifica Network Radio Los Angeles, and a weekly commentator on the Radio-One Network. He is also a guest MSNBC Political Analyst.

He is President of the Los Angeles Urban Policy Roundtable, a public charity, education and civic engagement organization.

Index

Made in the USA
Middletown, DE
03 February 2016